LIFE CHANGING JOURNEYS IN "UNIFIED CONSCIOUSNESS"

RIPPLING OUT FROM THE LAND OF RUMI

Esra Üstar Oğuz

BALBOA
PRESS
A DIVISION OF HAY HOUSE

Copyright © 2013 Esra Üstar Oğuz.

All rights reserved. No part of this book may be used or reproduced by any means, graphic, electronic, or mechanical, including photocopying, recording, taping or by any information storage retrieval system without the written permission of the publisher except in the case of brief quotations embodied in critical articles and reviews.

Balboa Press books may be ordered through booksellers or by contacting:

Balboa Press
A Division of Hay House
1663 Liberty Drive
Bloomington, IN 47403
www.balboapress.com
1-(877) 407-4847

Because of the dynamic nature of the Internet, any web addresses or links contained in this book may have changed since publication and may no longer be valid. The views expressed in this work are solely those of the author and do not necessarily reflect the views of the publisher, and the publisher hereby disclaims any responsibility for them.

The author of this book does not dispense medical advice or prescribe the use of any technique as a form of treatment for physical, emotional, or medical problems without the advice of a physician, either directly or indirectly. The intent of the author is only to offer information of a general nature to help you in your quest for emotional and spiritual well-being. In the event you use any of the information in this book for yourself, which is your constitutional right, the author and the publisher assume no responsibility for your actions.

Design Modification of the Dolphin Figure by:
Organik Tasarim - Ali Dogan, Turkey

Any people depicted in stock imagery provided by Thinkstock are models, and such images are being used for illustrative purposes only.
Certain stock imagery © Thinkstock.

Printed in the United States of America

ISBN: 978-1-4525-6966-6 (sc)
ISBN: 978-1-4525-6967-3 (e)

Library of Congress Control Number: 2013903795

Balboa Press rev. date: 04/08/2013

To those who resonate with the frequency of love …

TABLE OF CONTENTS

Preface ix
Acknowledgments xv
Chapter 1   Life Is Simple 1
Chapter 2   Speaking My Truth 9
Chapter 3   Connecting with Being 31
Chapter 4   Messages from the Animal Kingdom 39
Chapter 5   A Past Life Never Lies 47
Chapter 6   Self-Love.. 55
Chapter 7   Attitude of Gratitude..61
Chapter 8   Trusting Your Inner Voice 67
Chapter 9   Your Body Speaks to You 75
Chapter 10 Creating with Colors 81
Chapter 11 Your Intentions Orchestrate Your Life 91
Chapter 12 From the Angelic Realm 97
Chapter 13 Some Unusual Visits.. 105
Chapter 14 The Mystery of Dreams................................... 109
Afterword..113
Reading List.. 115
Works Cited 119

Preface

We live as ripples of energy in the vast ocean of energy.
—Deepak Chopra, *The Way of the Wizard:
Twenty Spiritual Lessons for Creating the Life You Want.*

I AM ON A lifelong quest for learning, both as a student and as a teacher. I am here to learn and share as I work toward my inner healing. My life is about flowing through intensive changes and transforming. My biggest transformation involves moving from the head to feelings, opening my heart to join the universal heart. In this book, I will detail step by step my journey on this quest.

I had always felt I was here for a purpose. I intuitively knew that this purpose was larger than I was. Many years ago, when I read about Carl Jung's theory of collective consciousness, I immediately embraced the concept. My inner wisdom instantly recognized the bigger picture and the interconnectedness of each human being, and I began to remember who I was.

I have kept a diary since my teenage years. Seeing the changes in my thoughts and feelings from one day to the next has always been fascinating. What I find important one day might be totally irrelevant and trivial the next day. Making a decision might be a nightmare at first, but the choice may become simple when I reconsider the situation the following day.

This inner dialogue over the years has inspired me to search beyond ever-shifting circumstances. I have always thought that there is more to life than what we experience with our five senses. My curiosity constantly pushed me to discover the orchestrating source behind the scenes.

When I reflect more deeply on my experiences, I realize how I continually managed to change and grow. I allowed myself to change even when my mind said, *I do not understand how it works.* I know that others can transform their lives once they allow themselves to change.

Each chapter in this book represents a major portal I have opened into my being as I moved on in life. I will openheartedly share my journey toward well-being, providing many tips I discovered along the way. Life is all about choices, the most important one being to consciously choose love over fear. Once you transcend fear, you can walk through the door. The journey starts with effortless little steps, which usually appear as simple, everyday choices. You must always ask yourself this question: Is my choice based on love or on fear?

*****

FROM THE DAY THAT I started to practice Dolores Cannon's Quantum Healing Hypnosis Therapy, I archived the voice recordings and analyzed them. During these extraordinary sessions, my clients can converse with their essences and are surprised at how they lose track of time and space. They choose words they would not normally use and speak in a different tone than they usually do.

I call myself the facilitator in this process, since I take them on a journey through their consciousness. This consciousness already knows why they came to me, and it takes them to just the right time and space to enable their transformation. I do not guide my clients but instead outline the overall process and help them flow with it. It is important that the process be clear from the start, since this allows clients to let go of the conscious mind and let the subconscious mind emerge more easily. My clients might experience past lives, visit important scenes from their current lives or parallel lives, and even have a glimpse of the future. It is all good.

With some of my clients, the sessions take another turn. The information gained is not solely about the client. Words of wisdom flow from a client's mouth, and I feel how we are connected to each other. A client will often answer a question before I pose it. Telepathy has always been part of these sessions. My clients speak with various beings, animals, guides, and angels. It is magical.

Let me define the terms *Superconscious* and *higher self*. The Superconscious is the unified field of intelligence (oneness). It is all knowing. The higher self (or subconscious) of human beings is connected to this field beyond space and time. All knowledge is accessible in this space beyond the physical. All conscious beings, not just humans, are part of this perfect puzzle and continually feed their experiences back to the source. As Vedic wisdom teaches, the Atman (conscious being) is a wave in the ocean of Brahman, the source or oneness.

As I continued my practice over the years, at one point the Superconscious said, "We share with you so much. You need to write these things down and share them with humanity." In a recent session, I asked if there was more they wanted to share, and they said, "No. Not now. There will be more for your next books." Mission completed!

The Turquoise Ripple is about effortless self-transformation. I speak from my heart center and give many life-changing examples, including those drawn from my own experience. I have observed that the intention to change is the trigger. Once the intention is set, all we need to do is stay aware and allow the transformation.

Turquoise means "Turkish" in French. It is a color deeply engraved in Turkish history, culture, and art. I am a native of Turkey, and we call turquoise "Turkish blue." I hope that through these writings, the world will accept my call for transcending limitations and embracing change, transformation, and unconditional love. My intention is that this call ripples out to the whole world.

According to many wisdom traditions, turquoise means being heart centered and speaking one's truth. Through its unique energy, this color helps to balance thoughts and emotions, recharge spirits during times of mental stress and fatigue, and open the door to spiritual growth. Turquoise represents open communication from and between the heart and the spoken word. It radiates the peace, calm, and tranquility of blue, the balance and growth of green, and the uplifting energy of yellow. It enhances the ability to focus and concentrate and assists with clear thinking and decision-making. It is calming yet invigorating, restoring depleted energies. It encourages inner healing by enhancing empathy and caring (Scott-Kemmis, Judy, 2012).

Since turquoise also heightens our intuitive ability and alleviates loneliness, it brings us closer to unity consciousness. As the Superconscious said during my practice, "You (light workers) will continue to grow in number and come together. The circle will grow bigger, like the ripple created by a pebble thrown in the water. It does not matter where you are in the circle. One vibration will affect the other, this earth, this universe, and others; one pebble is enough."

In this book, I first share my views on the wonders of life. Then I invite you to journey with me through my gradual transition from corporate life to practicing spiritual hypnotherapy. Such a dramatic shift was possible only after I learned to connect with my being. I learned to receive messages from the universe, which come in many forms. Experiencing past lives is a big component for me and my clients. Messages regarding the importance of gratitude and self-love, as well as listening to your inner voice and your body, are consistently communicated in our sessions. The key is to establish our intentions and recognize that we are cocreators of our lives.

The latter part of the book is about the initial contacts I made with the angelic realm and extraterrestrial beings. I have been interested in metaphysical matters for as long as I can remember. Through my practice, I am able to speak with beings from other realities, and I am infinitely grateful for this. It is my pleasure to share such mind-blowing stories with you.

I salute you with the compassion and wisdom of the heart, wishing that with each passing day you radiate more peace, harmony, laughter, and love.

My teacher Deepak Chopra says, "You will be transformed by what you read." I wholeheartedly hope that reading this book will be an effortless little step toward being you.

And please remember that all is always well.

Acknowledgments

I would like to express my deep gratitude to the key people in my life journey.

I would first like to thank my parents, grandparents, and sister for helping me be who I am.

I also would like to thank all my beloved teachers, particularly Gulgun Bakir, Yuksel Sokmen Ahmedoglu, Deepak Chopra, David Simon, and Dolores Cannon.

Last but not least, I would like to thank my very dear husband, who continues to graciously share his heart's wisdom and love during our journey of self-discovery.

Chapter 1

Life Is Simple

*Birdsong brings relief
To my longing.
I am just as ecstatic as they are,
But with nothing to say!
Please, universal soul, practice
Some song, or something, through me!*

—Rumi

This book is my song, which I am singing to you through written words.

I have written this book so that you can open any page at any time and be inspired to take an effortless little step to change yourself in any way you want. As Mahatma Gandhi said, "You must be the change you wish to see in the world." In my life's journey, I have discovered that just a word, a sentence, or a heartfelt sharing can magically resonate with another. Through such heart-to-heart connections, others are convinced that they can easily transform their lives. I have lived many such moments. I have seen friends, family, and clients experience phenomenal shifts. I sincerely hope that, through reading this book, you also will be inspired to bravely walk the path to reach your potential.

I have always believed in simplicity. This was clear when I started my work life, but looking back, I can see that I always valued this virtue. Last year, my yoga teacher, Vandana, who is of Indian origin, taught me some basic yoga positions in such simple ways that suddenly I had a realization: everything that is not simple is most likely bundled with ego! Ego tends to make things complicated. Simplicity, on the other hand, is very effective. Therefore I have chosen to make this a simple book for people to read and find tips about how to change their lives if they are called to do that.

Through years of practicing hypnotherapy, I found out that people always need to change. Whether the problem is big or small, something is always bugging them. Joy is somehow reduced in their lives. The discomfort might feel very small, or it might involve a big physical problem. People often look for quick ways to change, to leave behind something or even everything. I would like to show you how this is possible with simple, small steps. This is a very easy-to-read book. Its aim is to share with you effective tips to transform yourself and live a more joyful, effortless life.

Why, then, are people stuck? If life is so simple and change is so easy, what is the missing piece, the trick people haven't discovered?

The trick is to recognize the big picture, the one beyond the physical life that we experience with our five senses through the visible world. Seeing this starts with opening your mind to the possibility. Life is all about the use and manipulation of energy. Energy works on you, but you cannot see, touch, smell, hear, or taste it. However, you are inevitably a part of it! Once you recognize this bigger picture, you will find it much easier to identify and choose your path.

The energetic world is where everything happens, but we see energetic changes only when they create our reality. If you are unaware of the unseen plane of energy, you are more likely to feel stuck. Connecting the dots is difficult, since the information you have through your five senses is incomplete. You may exhaust all your brain's energy and still not find an explanation. For example, if you have an illness or an accident, you may struggle in vain to figure out why it happened.

Been there, done that!

I spent years trying to learn why people are the way they are and why things happen the way they do. My efforts produced no satisfactory explanation.

However, when I surrendered to discovering the unknown, I went through a huge paradigm shift. I realized that illnesses and accidents happen as a result of unbalanced energy. Such unbalanced, unhealthy energy accumulates over time and finally makes itself visible. This is a signal from the universe that you need to transform yourself quickly. Without change, bigger and stronger signals and messages will be on their way! It is time to seek your truth and find your path. Everyone has a unique path to walk.

�ххxx

ONE OF THE MAIN reasons people resist change is because they don't want to be forced from their comfort zones. Usually they are supporting others, and they feel sorrow or pity for close family members or friends. It is interesting that they feel those they help cannot do without them. Our sessions, like the one I will share in chapter 6, show that just the opposite is true— that people must help themselves and that the will to change can come only from within.

Recently, someone said to me, "Esra, I have a friend who needs this therapy very much but doesn't believe such change is possible. However, I still feel I should grab her and bring her to you. Do you think this would work?" I replied, "This is not how it works. People have free will, and you cannot and should not try to change anyone. All you have is yourself, and you must start the change there, taking even tiny steps, altering your energy field in such a way that the people around you will also start shifting and adapting—even without knowing it. Of course, it might come to a point where they separate their world from yours, and maybe that is best for everyone in the bigger picture."

I have found that detaching from the hardship and suffering of others is most difficult in parent-child relationships. During our sessions, each time we ask the Superconscious how we should better deal with our children or how we can ensure that they do what we feel is best, the answer is, "Just love them unconditionally and set them free." This answer indicates that the new age children (the so-called indigos, crystals, and rainbow children) have already arrived, fully adapted to the shifting consciousness. They have expanded awareness and are enlightened teachers. So we are the ones who have the harder task to accomplish in terms of adaptation and transformation. Therefore we are advised to set our children free and let them find their own paths.

Another obstacle is being mired in new age jargon and saddled with things we think we must do. These imperatives include checklists detailing how to ascend, how to clean karma, and how to have a wonderful *merkaba* (the energy body aligning mind, body, and heart). But we will not be able shift our awareness unless each of us takes this path. Ultimately, one can do nothing more for others than share experiences, which is my aim here. The shift in consciousness will not happen with knowledge or checklists. It is important to detach from all these prerequisites and avoid attending one course after another, constantly looking for your truth outside of yourself.

One of my favorite quotes is from Hermann Hesse's masterpiece *Siddhartha*. The title character tells a friend, "You, O worthy one, are perhaps indeed a seeker, for in striving toward your goal, you do not see many things that are under your nose." (Hesse, 108) You can certainly open key doors by getting information and help and experiencing energetic shifts while working with therapists and teachers who resonate with you. All this helps. Your awareness will be expanded, and you may start seeing familiar things differently. Then you are on your own in contemplating this new, elevated perspective, incorporating it into your life, and applying what you have learned. The process is all about experiencing and staying grounded. As the Superconscious always reminds us, "After your current life, you will come here anyway. Live your life there while you are there!"

Inner work awaits you here and now.

I have also seen clients who receive all the answers from the Superconscious (through our conversations with their higher selves), and as always, I ask them to go back and listen to the recordings of the sessions. But the next time we talk, I may learn that they have not done this. That is like hearing the answers, reaching that sacred space, but choosing not to do anything with those pearls of wisdom. We always have choices, don't we?

Another pitfall is doubts about the messages relayed during the sessions. I will always tell a client that no other human being could have seen, said, or experienced exactly the same things he did. Therefore this message is uniquely for him and from him. It is his own consciousness, his own energy talking. Still, people have free will to choose what to believe.

The doubting person might be someone you love very much, but it is still nearly impossible to make that person do or believe anything. You can only let the person be. To do otherwise may be counterproductive. For example, telling an overweight person not to eat too much might have the opposite effect. One of the biggest lessons learned in a recent session (detailed in chapter 8) was acceptance and trust. The Superconscious said, "If you do not accept things—in this case, the death of a much-loved brother in a past life—you cannot live with joy." We always think we know best, but the mind is actually setting traps to keep us captive.

Finally, a major reason people claim they cannot change is their genetic heritage. The gene myth is so much promoted that people easily give away their power, and in doing so, play the victim. To understand the fallacy of this myth, read (or listen to) Bruce Lipton. A biologist, he explains why we are free to change. He notes that "genes and DNA do not control our biology; that instead DNA is controlled by signals from outside the cell, including the energetic messages emanating from our positive and negative thoughts." In his groundbreaking book *The Biology of Belief,* he discusses the incredible power of the mind and details the insights on mind-body pathways that his research on cells has produced. He also discusses the conscious mind versus the subconscious mind (the basis for hypnosis). The conscious mind creates positive thoughts; the subconscious mind, however, is like a computer—it continues running programs, some implanted at conception. Emotions in the conscious mind produce signals that trigger the cells to do their work following subconscious programming.

Lipton's synthesis of the latest and best research in cell biology and quantum physics is being hailed as a major breakthrough showing that our bodies can be changed as we retrain our thinking. "We can control our lives by controlling our perceptions," he says.

"I was exhilarated by the new realization that I could change the character of my life by changing my beliefs," Lipton says. "I was instantly energized because I realized that there was a science-based path that would take me from my job as a perennial victim to my new position as cocreator of my destiny."

Deepak Chopra mentions in his lectures that 98 percent of the body renews itself within one year and the remaining 2 percent within two to three years. Echoing Lipton, he says, "You can free yourself from aging by reinterpreting your body and by grasping the link between belief and biology." He also says, "The physical world, including our bodies, is a response of the observer. We create our bodies as we create the experience of our world."

✽✽✽✽✽

I WOULD LIKE TO share some definitions that are at the core of my journey:

Consciousness is defined as awareness.

Its synonyms are cognizance, mindfulness, realization, and recognition.

Transformation is defined as complete change.

Once transformed, you cannot return to your previous state of being. Transformation is represented by the element of fire. It is said that Sufis burn with the fire of love. Sufism awakens the lamp of divine light within the heart.

Transformation's synonyms are metamorphosis, shift, switchover, and transmutation.

"According to Vedanta, there are only two symptoms of enlightenment, just two indications that a transformation is taking place within you toward a higher consciousness," Chopra says. "The first symptom is that you stop worrying. Things don't bother you anymore. You become lighthearted and full of joy. The second symptom is that you encounter more and more meaningful coincidences in your life, more and more synchronicities. And this accelerates to the point where you actually experience the miraculous."

✽✽✽✽✽

THIS BOOK IS ABOUT my song, my journey, and about sharing my experiences on this journey. It is written from my heart and includes highlights of the many hours of hypnotherapy sessions I have had with numerous clients over the years. I emphasize quality, not quantity, so it is short, direct, and selective. My aim is to spread the light I have discovered in myself and have helped others find in themselves. Reading this book, you will learn about the energy game and start to play it if you choose. I hope you will enjoy the game as much as I do. After all, this is why you chose to be here on Gaia right now—to create with her at this historically critical time of consciousness transformation.

Chapter 2

Speaking My Truth

Happiness is when what you think, what you say, and what you do are in harmony.

—Mahatma Gandhi

THE FIRST TIME I heard about "speaking your truth," I felt free as a bird.

I had nearly completed my thirteenth year in corporate life. I felt hollow, almost robotic. In fact, since the first days, corporate life felt confining. I felt I did not belong, but I did not know what to do about it.

I was recovering from a potentially fatal illness and starting to regularly practice Ashtanga yoga. I call this my first contact with my soul. So much was going on for me, both physically and emotionally.

I was looking back and trying to connect the dots. This nonstop process was very tiring. I kept asking, *Why did all this happen to me? What did I do wrong? And more important, what should I do now? Is there any hope of turning my life around?*

I have been a very curious person all my life. Seeing behind people and events was something of a hobby. I was particularly drawn to deep subjects that were not easily comprehensible at first glance. Because I was always hungry for knowledge, I read, researched, studied, and learned extensively. Reading one book after another made life bearable for me, since this opened the doors to other people's lives. I hoped to find the truth by reading about others' experiences. What else was there to do?

Gaining knowledge is certainly key to knowing oneself, but the journey within is largely an experiential process. Everyone has his own path to walk and his own choices to make along this path. Just as no two pieces of turquoise have the same pattern, each of us is unique. We can explore that individuality.

We are here to live and to learn.

Experiencing Corporate Life

LIKE MOST PEOPLE, I was brought up in an achievement-oriented environment. I was born in Istanbul, Turkey, and I attended a competitive American high school and university there. I majored in business administration.

I worked part time while studying at the university. A strong voice inside me kept saying that the real world was out there and not in additional degrees at school. I was able to squeeze in a great deal while studying and working. Meeting new people was the real bonus. I worked with tourist guides, top-level executives, owners of public relations agencies, high-flying managers at top audit firms and banks, musicians, photographers, and accountants. With the extra cash, I joined and led international volunteer work camps in Turkey and in Europe through a youth organization called Genctur.

Though I knew what I did not want to do, I had no clue what I wanted to do!

I saw that managing time and recognizing priorities were the ways to optimize life. I had to do my best at this or I would fall behind in the race. I knew that I needed to keep ahead of the game as much as possible.

One day during my senior year at the university, my father handed me an ad he had cut out from a local newspaper. It read,

"European Financial Seminar in Paris." Knowing I loved to travel, he thought I would be interested in this chance to visit Paris at no cost. Procter & Gamble was offering the seminar and inviting students to go through an intensive interview process. I immediately accepted the challenge and was on my way to Paris six months later.

That week in Paris was a once-in-a-lifetime adventure. Two dozen top students from twelve countries were selected to attend the event. We all had great ambition, but my expectations were low. I was simply enjoying the trip. Shortly after returning home, I was offered a job as a financial analyst. I had officially kicked off my nineteen-year corporate career.

During the interviews, I was asked the cliché question, "Why should we select you?" I thought for a few moments and then replied, "Perhaps I can look at things differently than you." I intuitively felt that the company was hindered by too many templates and that such a giant worldwide conglomerate always needed fresh blood. This is exactly how I feel about the world today, and that is why I have written this book in which I share awakenings to my truth through a series of synchronicities.

From the moment we are born to the time of our transition, we have endless opportunities in front of us. Our souls choose just the right pathways for our evolution. You may ask how I am so sure, and if I am right, what is the guiding star to follow to take these opportunities.

The answer from the Superconscious is that, "All you need to do is to stay awake and follow the signs." In the chapters to come, I will share many highlights of how this happened.

※※※※※

IN THAT THIRTEENTH YEAR of my corporate life, I was working at Cisco, another giant multinational company. After working for eight years at Procter & Gamble in the fast-moving consumer goods industry, I had switched to the information technology field. I was in my fifth year at Cisco and struggling to keep interested in my work. I was changing assignments every one and a half to two years. Constant change of focus, teams, and goals kept me going throughout my career. I also had to travel a lot in Europe and overseas and this made life bearable. But I kept asking myself, *What will happen to end this monotonous misery?* I knew deep inside that I could not go on living in the same way. The universe started to show me the signs right away.

First, I sprained my ankle on a business trip to Paris, and shortly after, I had a serious eye infection. However, I still did not reduce my workload. I managed to work on my computer with only one eye open! Later on, I learned that my body was crying out for attention because it was in deep pain. My energetic body was so stressed that I was manifesting this pain in the physical realm.

Because I did not stop to listen, a third manifestation knocked on my door. On a business trip to Athens, a colleague noticed a mole on my upper left arm and said that I should get it checked. Shortly after, I was diagnosed with melanoma, the most dangerous form of skin cancer. I had two operations within two weeks. My world was shattered. Introspection was inescapable now. I had three main regrets. I asked myself, *Why do I do nothing but work and fail to take more time to enjoy myself? Why do I always save for the future although I can never know how much of a future I have? Why don't I travel as much as I want, always postponing the trips I hope to take?*

I had to start from scratch and build a life that worked for me. Whatever the cost, I knew that I had to speak my truth at all times. Life was passing me by!

Searching for Answers

DEEPAK CHOPRA SAYS, "WHEN the pain of being the same becomes greater than the pain of being different, you change." I surely was at that point in my life.

Thus came deep soul searching. I needed to speak my truth, but where and how would I find it?

I started practicing the timeless yogic positions in a class twice a week. These hours were the only times when I felt no competition, when I had to be no one but myself. As my body relaxed, my mind relaxed and let go. What a gift that was just to be thoughtless or beyond thought! I can see now that these were my first experiences beyond time and space. This was my awakening to present-moment awareness. Where there was no past, there was no conditioning, and where there was no future, there were no worries. According to the timeless teachings of Vedanta, this is the area of pure potentiality. Experiencing this stillness brings one in touch with the soul. In his lectures, Chopra quotes Krishna in the Bhagavad Gita as saying about the soul, "Water cannot wet it, wind cannot dry it, weapons cannot shatter it, fire cannot burn it, because it's ancient, it's unborn, and it can never die."

The major step toward opening my heart and beginning to speak my truth was learning to meditate. Meditation brought outstanding clarity to my thinking, which triggered a quantum leap in my creativity. Being more creative, I was more productive and efficient at everything I did.

"There are three ways of understanding reality," says Chopra. "The least reliable is through the eye of the flesh, or seeing through our five senses. Till recently, science was an extension of the eye of the flesh. The second way, which is a little deeper, is through the eye of the mind. If I want to understand the Pythagoras theorem, quantum physics or the theory of relativity, I have to know the principles of Euclidean geometry or mathematics that exist only in the mind. That takes me a little deeper into the heart of nature's secrets. And the third way is through the eye of the soul. That takes us really into the heart and soul of reality." (Life Positive, 2000)

I have found that the eye of the soul is accessible when meditating in complete silence. It is no coincidence that all great sages and thinkers, regardless of what age they lived in or what beliefs they held, have recommended this practice as a way to transcend the illusion created by the mind. Once our physical eyes are closed, the heart space blooms through the outlet created. Opening the heart is simply connecting to your essence, and it is extremely rewarding. It is as if you are diving into yourself and hugging yourself in deep longing. Some months ago, I was practicing inspirational writing following meditation. I asked, *How can I further open my heart?* I clearly saw the vision of a dolphin diving into the ocean and felt as if I were plunging into my heart. The experience was powerful and emotional. There are no words to describe it. I will talk more about inspirational writing in chapter 8.

As I began to speak my truth with my family, friends, colleagues, and managers, my life started to flow more smoothly. Any day that I was not going to the hospital for an operation was already a perfect one, so nothing could spoil it. I became very brave and took bold steps in terms of deciding which assignments to accept at work, who to hire for my team, and which business trips to make. I became a master of knowing exactly when to say yes and how to say no.

A milestone was when I chose not to attend a mandatory conference overseas. My only major worry was the reaction of a company vice president, who might ask why I didn't go. I took the risk of being challenged and possibly weakening my reputation for always being available. I went on official leave and attended an angelic reiki course in the UK that a friend was teaching. I had no idea what I was doing, but I knew I had to dare to live.

A few months later, I had to face the much-dreaded question from the vice president over the phone, and I was amazed at how smoothly the discussion went.

"Esra," he said, "I did not see you at the conference."

"Yes, indeed. I could not make it. And do you know why?"

"No. Why?"

"Oh, so you have not heard that on my previous trip to that city, we went through a very disturbing emergency landing. I could not convince myself to go there again. I have caught up with all the information I needed though, so all is well."

"Oh, sorry to hear about the landing trouble," he said. "Okay then. What about your next assignment?"

Can you imagine how happy I felt at that moment? I knew that I had the power and that I could exercise my free will even in a very competitive corporate environment. I just had to speak my truth!

Training to be an angelic reiki master proved to be a landmark in shifting realities. A friend of mine was teaching this method and had invited me to stay at her house for the course. All was a blur for me at that moment. I had taken a Usui reiki course in Istanbul, but had not changed much in my life. It just was an interesting experience and a chance to meet new people. However, I had felt little in my heart or soul.

Angelic reiki was completely different. Throughout the course and especially when we were practicing on each other, a great deal was going on in my body. For the first time I saw colors with my third eye. I learned to recognize my feeling body, experienced attunements, and practiced looking at life in a nonanalytical way. I learned that there are no coincidences and that there is a reason for every feeling. It is very important to relax!

Following this training, from time to time I have practiced angelic reiki on myself and love it. What I enjoy the most is that I ask questions and my body answers immediately. When I fully relax, let go, and ask for help from the angels, I feel the healing in a short while. That is amazing. I always ask that the energy go wherever it is needed most. It is also amazing how the body knows better than the mind. I expect heat and tingling in one part of my body, but feel it elsewhere! Afterward, I realize that was where I needed those sensations most. I accept this as a new language, one full of symbols and mysteries.

This training opened the door for me to communicate with my body. In chapter 9, I will discuss how the body talks to us.

Inner Knowingness and Awareness Shift

Even though my work life was far more effective, rewarding, and smooth, I began to say, *I will have a second life after forty*. I am not exactly sure how this idea grew in me, but I somehow knew it like I knew my name. Today, when I look back, I call this "inner knowingness." I later learned that countless people, including prophets and wise ones, had their biggest awakenings around this age and made great contributions to the world. I may have picked up this idea from the Superconscious or the collective unconscious without recognizing it.

All corporate jobs were repetitious and routine to me, simply more of the same and pretty draining, too. Time spent on travel, meetings, conference calls, coaching, and delegating was still a huge chunk of my life.

As I was juggling my work life with these conflicting thoughts, I went to the Italian Alps for a short holiday. During that week, I read two books that completely transformed my life for different but complementary reasons. The first was Carl Johan Calleman's *The Mayan Calendar and the Transformation of Consciousness* and the second was Mirzakarim Norbekov's *The Experience of a Fool Who Had an Epiphany about How to Get Rid of His Glasses*.

Calleman's book was quite a shock. Reviewing the historical

facts outlined and learning about the spiral nature of time and events, I realized that we were living in an extremely special age. We had to wake up and see the bigger picture as soon as possible and catch up with the consciousness shift that had been taking place for decades! My whole being wanted to be totally free to pursue the path of enlightenment, and I did not want to waste another day in corporate life. Reality as we know it would soon be shattered, so it made no sense to continue what I was doing. On the other hand, it was fantastic to discover that there was a bright future for awakened humans, who could shift with the transforming earth. Realizing this filled some of the hollowness in me.

Norbekov's book is about manifesting physical, mental, and emotional healing through the power of the mind. Its roots go back to Joseph Murphy's *The Power of Your Subconscious Mind*. This groundbreaking professor deepened that earlier wisdom through years of research. Norbekov holds that with concentrated attention and use of the body's bioenergy, it is possible to remember the healthy state we were in at birth. The principle is that wherever attention goes, energy flows. Learning and practicing this method at ten-day seminars held in Istanbul, I healed my eyes from farsightedness, and astigmatism and stopped wearing glasses. This made me believe that I could do anything I wanted. I experienced how my consciousness manifested my physical reality and how the bioenergy of the body could be channeled for self-healing. I learned to talk to my body and to apologize when needed. Finally, I started to accept and love myself, experiencing moments of deep forgiveness and compassion.

The great emotional release I felt at these seminars made it clear that I was on a different life path. The joy of seeing people freed from emotional baggage and completely healed of serious chronic illnesses like diabetes was overwhelming. I wanted to be in environments where people were improving their quality of life. I wanted to work for the well-being of others and in harmony with them. I deeply felt and enjoyed the high energy, satisfaction, and happiness in such environments. These were places where people cared for each other. This was the heart-centered approach to life that has become my passion and mission.

11:11

During these seminars, other signs came pouring in. I read Dan Millman's *The Life You Were Born to Live*. Numbers had been dear to my heart since my school days, and now they had even deeper meaning for me. I learned the science of numerology, and it still dominates my communication with the universe and deepens my understanding of the flow of life. If I did not discuss in greater detail the profound effect numbers have had on me, my story would not be complete.

Just like every word, each digit has a unique vibrational energy. And just as words we read or hear carry meaning, each number pops up into our lives with messages of its own. This feels purely magical. Let me share with you how numbers showed themselves to me.

I heard about the 11:11 phenomenon during a summer vacation on Turkey's Aegean coast. I was totally skeptical and said, "It should be a coincidence, nothing more."

On the Sunday that I returned from the vacation, I woke up early in the morning, meditated, and did housework. I looked at the digital clock on my bedside and saw "11:11." I softly smiled and thought, "How cool." Following a busy day, I tidied up the house, took a shower, and sat on my bed. I turned my head and saw the clock. It read, "11:11."

This was unbelievable. What could account for such a coincidence, seeing the same time to the minute on the same day? This was beyond the mind's grasp.

After this, the phenomenon attracted my attention more often and in an expanded way. My eyes caught twenty-twos, thirty-threes, and forty-fours on the clock and on license plates. The numbers kept jumping out when I watched TV or videos. They appeared anywhere, anytime without warning! When I stayed at a hotel, the floor number or the room number would have elevens in it or would add up to eleven or a multiple of eleven. Probably the best way to put it is to say that numbers happen to you.

As my awareness increased, I could clearly get the messages from the universe. When I was making decisions about buying or selling something, hiring people, or going somewhere, my eyes would somehow "unconsciously" gaze at the clock and see the message there. It is important to note that if you try to catch these numbers, you can't! Your energy will merge with the energy of these meaningful numbers only when you let go of thoughts and expectations. When this happens, I feel that I am aligned with the flow of life. In a recent hypnotherapy session, my therapist asked why I was seeing these numbers so often. The answer was that, "It is reassurance of the big picture and the oneness and that I am here only temporarily."

Oneness, as I learned while studying Vedic wisdom at Chopra Center University, is the ocean, and the life of a human being is like a wave in that ocean. We are born, and the wave rises. We experience life and return to oneness; then the wave disappears back into the ocean. This also wonderfully explains our connectedness—the collective consciousness, the Superconscious, telepathy, channeling, remote viewing, and how several scientists come up with the same discovery at the same time unaware of each other. The unified field of intelligence is the key to playing the energy game here on earth.

For me, the number eleven has even bigger importance, since my life path number is eleven. If you add the digits of your birthday one by one, you will arrive at your own number. Just add the resulting digits until you get one digit only. If you get master numbers like eleven, twenty-two, or thirty-three, the number's effect is doubled, meaning that it is even stronger. In my case, the energy of the number one is doubled.

This number is about creativity and confidence. As I read Millman's book, it occurred to me that I could be more successful in corporate life, but I would definitely lack satisfaction. It was quite a shock, and I knew that I needed to change direction.

✻✻✻✻✻

So what does seeing 11:11 mean in general? Why do millions of people around the world see these numbers? The best explanation I have found is from Uri Geller, who says on his Web site, "The endless reoccurrence of these hours 11:11, 11:01, 11:10, 10:01, 10:11, 10:10, 1:01, 1:11 represents a positive connection and a gateway to the mysteries of the universe and beyond." He calls this a "trigger of remembrance" and says that "the sightings of 11:11 tend to occur during times of heightened awareness, having a most powerful effect on the people involved. The appearance of 11:11 is also a powerful confirmation that we are on the right track, aligned with our highest Truth."

Geller says that "11:11 is a pre-encoded trigger placed into our cellular memory banks prior to our descent into matter which, when activated, signifies that our time of completion is near. This refers to the completion of duality. When 11:11 appears to you, it is your wake-up call. A direct channel opens up between you and the Invisible. When this happens, it is time to reflect on whatever you are doing for a moment and Look Larger. You can enter the Greater Reality if you wish pray or meditate and seed your future and also, you can be seeded by the Invisible. You can ask for help in some specific area of your life or simply listen quietly and receive a revelation. The appearance of 11:11 is an always-beneficial act of Divine Intervention telling you that it is time to take a good look around you and see what is really happening beyond the veils of illusion. You are ready to step into the Greater Reality, ascending from duality into Oneness, into Love. The Doorway, the 11:11 can presently be perceived as a crack between two worlds. It is like a bridge, which has the inherent potential of linking together two very different spirals of energy. Thus this bridge functions as an invisible door, a doorway into the Invisible realm, to an entirely different spiral of evolution. The 11:11 has rested dormant within us since that faraway position under time-release mechanization, combined with sealed orders which would only open when the 11:11 was fully activated. It has been gently sleeping, awaiting the moment of triggering. And now the 11:11 is finally activated ... 11 is 1+1, equaling 2, which symbolizes unity, togetherness, peace." (Geller, 1998)

As Chopra says, "The direction of life is from duality to unity."

Experiencing No Time, No Space

DURING THOSE YEARS, I had heard of a psychic lady with shamanic education who was channeling her clients' spirit guides and helping to find answers to their challenges and to heal them. All this was done over the phone, a no-space, no-time exercise. One day, just before I was starting class with my loving pilates teacher, yet another person mentioned this healer's name. This was a clear sign from the universe, since I had been pondering whether to give this healing modality a chance. It was clear that I was not finding a way out of my unsatisfying life on my own. Though I had recovered from my earlier illness, I now had fibromyalgia, the reason for personal physical training twice a week. Although these hours were relaxing and healing, my body was still crying out and saying, "You have unresolved matters lingering over you!"

Taking the road less traveled (the title of Scott Peck's stellar book), I started to work with this gifted lady and peel the onion layer by layer. The energetic planes revealing why things were manifesting as they did were completely and shockingly different from what we experience through our worldly eyes. Working with my gentle spiritual healer felt as if I had started a new school. This healer's ability to read me like a book was mind-boggling. The topic that came up repeatedly during these sessions was opening my heart. This appeared to be a compelling need for my soul, since I was struggling to find my way out of conditioning, judgment, and the ever-discriminating intellect. I was discovering the path of unconditional self-love. Faced with decisions big or small, I started asking, *Does this expand or shrink me?* and *Do I want to respond to this low energy or stay in higher energy?* These hourly sessions over the phone made a radical difference in my life. I was again beyond time and space, beyond the mind!

The concept of going beyond the mind attracted me so much that during one of these sessions, I was guided to discover hypnosis. Within a few days, more signs arrived. A business associate of my husband gave us a book on hypnosis. Then a magazine with an intriguing article on hypnosis appeared on my husband's desk at work. Finally, I sat down at my computer to search for a good school. I decided in less than an hour. "The law of least effort" was at work! A few months later, my husband and I got our certification from the Northern College of Therapeutic Hypnosis at Leeds University in England.

During this period, Chopra had come to Istanbul to give a speech. We attended his conference and admired his inspiring and enlightening presentation. Some months after this, we took a private lesson and learned to practice Primordial Sound Meditation as revived and modernized by Chopra and David Simon, founders of the Chopra Center in Carlsbad, California.

The technique is based on the ancient Vedic traditions of India. It is practiced by repeating the primordial sound mantra given to each person at a sacred, one-to-one ceremony. During the ritual, the teacher sings a beautiful ancient chant. This is a very powerful experience. The mantra is chosen through Vedic astrology and is calculated based on a person's place, date, and time of birth. Primordial sounds are vibrations of the universe, and they have the effect of drawing one's awareness to the gap between thoughts where there is no time or space.

Only eight months after learning it, my husband and I became certified instructors of this method and the timeless teachings on which it is built. It took us about six months of deep study. We spent many weeks in Carlsbad, attending courses on perfect health and the seduction of spirit. The week leading up to graduation included day after day of presentations and many written and oral exams. Everything flowed smoothly. As they say at Chopra University, "If you want to learn something well, be a teacher of that subject!"

Initially I thought it was not for me, but my husband was determined to become an instructor. I was fed up with studying, delivering presentations, and following schedules. We were already traveling to the UK every other week to learn the basics of hypnosis. On one of those trips, we were at the airport and I turned on my mobile phone briefly before boarding. I normally would not have done this, since it was very early in the morning. A new e-mail said, "Seduction of Spirit, a six-day meditation retreat." This suddenly shifted my view on becoming an instructor. I could attend this course and decide later whether to be an instructor. I registered.

The course was a mega experience. Meditating with more than four hundred like-minded people is not easy to describe. Listening to the many lectures by Chopra and Simon was enlightening, empowering, and fun. Doing yoga twice a day was nurturing. I felt at home; I wanted to stay at the Chopra Center forever.

At the end of the retreat, I knew I wanted to learn more and teach others this sacred wisdom. We stayed for another week, doing an Ayurvedic detox. This involved a week of holistic cleansing and healing, working at all levels—mind, body, spirit, and emotions.

�֍✾✾✾✾

MEDITATION IS AN INWARD journey of self-expansion, healing, and transformation. As long as the process is easy and effortless and comes with no expectations attached, it is perfect for the mind, body, and soul. To me, it is the sacred portal to finding happiness, fulfillment, and approval inside, not outside. As Rumi beautifully puts it,

> *I have lived on the lip of insanity,*
> *Wanting to know the reasons.*
> *Knocking on a door, it opens.*
> *I have been knocking from the inside!*

Realizing that all answers are within is an amazing discovery. But we must stop to listen to our inner voice, heard through the heart. Our minds must be the servants of the heart, or life will be a never-ending stream of conflicting thoughts.

Without clarity of mind and the peaceful, nonjudgmental space created by meditation, I could never have realized that we are not our thoughts, our bodies, our possessions, or our positions. The key to experiencing this space is to take our awareness from activity to the quieter levels of the mind until we slip beyond thought into silence. As the ninth-century sage Adi Shankara beautifully outlines in his "Layers of Life" diagram, we are timeless and limitless as long as we are aware that the subtle body (the mind, the ego, and the intellect) is the bottleneck. In silence, we can joyously experience our soul embracing our causal body (personal, collective, and finally universal consciousness), the area of wisdom and creativity. In silence, we also can effortlessly draw in the much-needed healing and rejuvenation energy from the vital force, the source. As Rumi says, "In this world of trickery, emptiness is what your soul wants." He advises that we let go and completely surrender to nothingness. Well, as much as we can!

The mechanics of living were becoming clearer to me day by day, and these teachings gave me hope for rebuilding a healthy and satisfying life. Well-being had a definition for me now, and it did not involve materiality, but purpose, service, and love. Asking the soul questions prior to meditating every day, I started a deeper conversation with the universe.

Who am I?

What do I really want?

What is my purpose in life? How can I help, how can I serve humanity?

My desires were being fulfilled with little effort, and life became more magical as I experienced higher states of consciousness. Beyond the usual sleeping, dreaming, and waking states, there is a whole new world of multiple realities. Passing through the sacred portal of meditation on a regular basis, experiencing cosmic, divine, and ultimately universal consciousness becomes possible. As I practiced switching to witnessing awareness (looking at myself from an elevated perspective, as a witness), synchronicities flourished even more in my life. The universe was orchestrating miraculous events, and it was quite a show!

Storm of Synchronicities

Perhaps the most amazing synchronicity (or meaningful

coincidence) of my life has been listening to Dolores Cannon on Kala Ambrose's "Explore Your Spirit with Kala" radio show. Late one evening, I clicked on the podcast "Convoluted Universe, with Dolores Cannon." I had no clue about her or any of her books, but when Cannon spoke, I came alive. She seemed to have all the answers and to know everything. I asked my husband to listen, and he was excited, too. He said, "You should get trained by her." I thought this was an unlikely possibility, since I was still in the corporate world and was already going to San Diego, California, for graduation week of the course on Primordial Sound Meditation instruction. I could not think of a way to meet her, since she was traveling extensively and teaching all around the world. I asked my husband to search the Internet and see if she were teaching anytime soon. I will always remember when he woke me up in the wee morning hours and said, "You won't believe it. Dolores is teaching the three days right before our graduation week! And guess where? In San Diego!"

The universe had already made the plan; we only had to notice it and pursue the unique opportunity.

The signs and synchronicities accelerated thereafter. Although all the logistics were perfectly planned for our trip, a volcano erupted in Iceland that week. We had our suitcases packed and ready at the door, but no flights were available. It felt surreal! Waiting more than three days, we were lucky enough to get the last two seats on a Lufthansa flight to San Diego, just in time for Cannon's level-one class.

My husband and I had a memorable moment before that last window of opportunity to take the class. We had completely surrendered and were meditating together. We really wanted to go, but we were totally helpless. Our contact at the travel agency suddenly called and said, "There are two last tickets for that flight. If you leave right now, you will make it in time!" Hearing the news, we almost levitated with joy and speeded to the airport.

On the plane, I was listening to a show that Ambrose did with Wendy Craig-Purcell, the founder of the Unity Church in San Diego. I was not aware of the coincidence that Craig-Purcell was based in San Diego. I was impressed by her loving words and her wisdom. A few days after we arrived, friends of my husband took us out for dinner. At one point, one of them said, "We have a whole new window in our life now. We are going to the Unity Church on Sundays!"

I was stunned. I quickly searched my short-term memory and said, "Purcell?"

They were shocked that I knew the name. That Sunday, we all went to listen to her, introduced ourselves, and told her our story. She was happy and excited. When we mentioned that we were there for the graduation week of Chopra's meditation course, she said, "Oh, please give him my regards. I just did a talk with him last week!" So now we had a mission, which was to meet Chopra and pass on Craig-Purcell's greeting.

Meeting Chopra was no piece of cake, since he quietly comes to a class and leaves in the same humble way. However, the universe had arranged another synchronicity for us. On the last day of our stay in Carlsbad, we were preparing to dine with the same friends. We left our room and were crossing the narrow street to get to the car park, and there he was, Deepak Chopra himself, on his evening walk! After introducing ourselves in great excitement, we mentioned Ambrose and Craig-Purcell. This was the climax of our trip.

Becoming a Dedicated Hypnotherapist

AFTER COMPLETING OUR INITIAL study of therapeutic hypnosis at Leeds University, we were looking to learn and practice at a deeper level. Traditional hypnosis meant a series of sessions, usually hourly, at which the client would be helped through the use of various suggestions. Dolores Cannon's Quantum Healing Hypnosis, however, was a single deep dive for as many hours as it took, usually around four. Rather than the alpha level (a light, meditative trance state), she works in the deeper theta state (experienced right before falling into deep sleep or just when waking up). Working with thousands of people, she discovered that what Carl Jung calls the collective unconscious is reachable in this state.

Talking to a person in this trance state is like talking to an all-knowing being beyond space and time. Moreover, and very significantly, this being, which Cannon calls the subconscious (I prefer the words *higher self* or *Superconscious*), knows all there is to know about this person and also anything and everything! Loving, sometimes authoritarian, and sometimes quite humorous, the higher self knows exactly what the person needs to know, see, and experience during the session. Its wisdom is such that the energy puzzle we cannot see with our minds is easily explained to the person in the most transformative ways possible. The only requirement of the person is to relax and allow, trusting the inner wisdom, which is one with the universal mind (or the unified field of intelligence).

What is amazing is that even in lighter states of trance, my clients easily experience past lives, and we can talk to their higher selves smoothly. Their voices change considerably, and when the Superconscious is speaking, the tone is like that of a totally different being. This all-knowing being usually speaks as *we,* and refers to the client lying on the bed as *he* or *she*. If you are familiar with channeling, you know what I mean. In each session, I explain to my clients, "If you went to a psychic, the information received through the psychic would first go through that person's consciousness and then on to you. In this session, you will be your own channel, getting information directly through your own consciousness, your own essence. Enjoy the amazing ride and appreciate the precious connection!"

Because many of my clients start forgetting the details of the session the minute they emerge from the trance, I do a voice recording of the session. I give a copy to the client and save the original for myself. The sessions from which I share highlights in this book are all archived in my records.

Since retiring early from corporate life, I have practiced this very effective hypnotherapy method. I also write and speak about the messages the Superconscious asks me to share with humanity. I initially started to share on Cannon's Quantum Healing Hypnosis Forum and was selected the Highlighted Dedicated Practitioner of Summer 2012 by Cannon and her team. I was honored that they recognized my contributions. It was a pleasure to share my experiences with my colleagues, especially the new practitioners.

We are living in special times, and it is my duty and privilege to share this work with you. As I learned to speak my truth and to open my heart, I shifted tracks and now feel that I am doing what I came here to do, living the life I chose to live. In ancient Vedic wisdom, this is called one's *dharma*, simply meaning "life purpose." Whether my journey resonates with you entirely or not much at all, I hope that you share the joy of the roller coaster I continue to ride.

One point regarding the hypnotherapy sessions is particularly important. Confidentiality is a major element of my practice, and I deeply respect my clients. All healing is based on trust and open communication. Therefore the names in this book are not the real names of my clients. All names are modified. Moreover, I have made every effort to leave out any personal information while still sharing the highlights of the sessions. I am deeply honored to have worked with every one of my clients. And as I always do after each session, I again thank them and their higher selves for their cooperation.

Chapter 3

Connecting with Being

Ever felt an angel's breath in the gentle breeze? A teardrop in the falling rain? Hear a whisper amongst the rustle of leaves? Or been kissed by a lone snowflake? Nature is an angel's favorite hiding place.

—Carrie Latet

PROBABLY ONE OF THE easiest, quickest, and most wonderful ways to change (or simply to change wavelength) and to get away from wherever you are in this cycle of life is going to nature. We hear this a lot, but do we put aside time for that? If so, do we do this regularly? The usual answer is no. We plan the time to have a picnic, take a walk, or go on a vacation, but that does not suffice.

One way to connect with nature is simply to look at a fresh flower in your own house! If you do not have a terrace or a garden, you can always grow a small plant somewhere in your house. Connecting with the plant, talking to it, or just looking at it will immediately bring you to a different level of awareness. If you cannot do this, buying fresh flowers is a good alternative. As Rumi's father Bahauddin says in *The Drowned Book,* "Flowers know without subject-object duality." (Barks, Moyne, XXiii) This means flowers carry the magic to bring you to the present moment where there is no separation, no good or bad, right or wrong, and thus no duality. Such judgment comes only from past conditioning or future worry.

You may ask yourself, *What is wrong with this moment?* The honest answer is "Nothing!" says Eckhart Tolle in his youtube videos. The energy field, the form, and the fragrance of flowers simply carry you away. You disconnect from your never-ending thoughts at least temporarily. "The gap between the thoughts is where there is endless possibility, or pure potentiality," Deepak Chopra explains in his lectures.

I once worked with a therapist who had a shamanic background, and I asked him, "What should I do when I feel disconnected and depressed?" He told me, "Just buy yourself fresh flowers." I was quite disappointed at his answer, since I was expecting to hear something like, "Read this book, then study this, and take that workshop." Our minds need to think, plan, and do things, when all we need is simply to be. During a recent hypnotherapy session at which I was the subject, my higher self (or subconscious) said, "Do less; be more." How wise to remember this when we are trying to squeeze too many activities into our already busy schedules!

*****

As you can imagine, because of my love for nature, I like taking walks in the forest where I am very lucky to live. I have always loved being alone in nature. The American high school where I studied from ages eleven through eighteen was in the woods, and I would always go there, even many years after my graduation, anytime I needed peace of mind. I would gaze at the Bosporus, close my eyes, and feel the grass under my palms while leaning against a big tree. This was the best of the best for me. Here I could view the Asian side of Istanbul from the hills of Europe. Istanbul is a unique city, with land on two continents.

I dictated these words into a voice recorder from the forest where I live. Always remember to connect with nature at least once a day. You will find that this becomes a wonderful habit. Looking at flowers and plants, touching them, and enjoying their fragrance will bring you to a new level without your knowing it. This is all part of the energy game.

Although I adore nature in any form, trees are my favorite. When I walk through the forest, I feel like swimming through the emerald green wave of trees, and this lifts my spirit every time. What I find amazing is that each moment in nature has a unique spark. I am in a trance state when strolling in the forest. Just the other day, a squirrel rushed onto the road to grab a tiny pinecone, and caught my glazed eyes. My mood shifted to joy in no time, and I wished I could hold on to that feeling forever.

I recently heard a character in a film say, "I knew it unconsciously before I knew it consciously." You will notice that you are being guided toward nature. Doors will open, bringing you to nature much more often than you thought possible. You will notice that your awareness of nature is increasing, and slowly, like me, you will start talking to plants and animals and hearing them respond. (My first short story was dictated to me by trees as I was walking in the forest.) This requires uninterrupted silence, which brings me to another tip about how you can connect to yourself.

❋❋❋❋❋

> *Out beyond ideas of wrong-doing and right-doing there is a field. I'll meet you there.*
>
> —Rumi

As I mentioned in Chapter 2, meditation is a key method for reaching a light, calm state. Like *love, meditation* is a word overused in our age. You might react to the word with indifference, but all wise ones have pointed to this practice as a sacred path to turn within. I had read many books, trying to learn the essentials of meditation. Nothing resonated with me until I discovered Chopra's scientifically tested method, built on Vedic wisdom. I suggest you learn meditation from a qualified instructor. The fundamentals can be summarized in this advice: doing keeps you in your mind and thoughts, so close your eyes, and experience silence. Do this when you wake up in the morning, and again in the evening. Your soul, your inner self, will be so happy to connect with you that you will start waking up earlier or putting aside more time before you go to sleep to enjoy this easy, gentle practice. In that sacred space, there are no worries, just a peaceful state of being.

Closing your eyes (immediately eliminating 40 percent of the distractions in your environment), and gently breathing into your belly is already relaxing. Thoughts will come, especially at the start, because the mind attempts to keep you busy and make you like a leaf in the wind. The brain does not rest when we sleep. We dream, and we go on solving everyday problems. While in corporate life, I would wake up in the middle of the night, write notes, and fall back to sleep (if I was lucky). Clearly, we need a way to relieve the busy brain, which might initially resist change. The longer you stay with yourself and sit in acceptance, letting thoughts come and go, the more you will notice that you are without conscious knowledge, almost becoming another person. You will find yourself in the space between thoughts, which is called the gap. This is where past conditioning dissolves and future worries are vaporized. Here you are a true human being.

When Siddhartha speaks to Buddha, he says, "Through a small gap, there streams into the world of unity something strange, something new, something that was not there before and that cannot be demonstrated and proved: that is your doctrine of raising above the world, of salvation." (Hesse, 27) Hermann Hesse explains that logic is broken at this point; this state is beyond teachings, but is still built on knowledge and then experienced.

※※※※※

THE MORE I OPENED up to my emotions, the more I adored the sea. In the past, I did not see the point in swimming, *Why get wet?* I thought. The more I relaxed, the more I wanted to be close to the sea or the ocean. Feeling the oneness was possible only when I surrendered to my feelings. I found out that this was typical; more sensitive and open people loved the sea, since they felt the emotional body of Gaia. They had no fear of connecting to their emotions.

Masaru Emoto has provided probably the most amazing scientific proof of the link between water and consciousness. The Japanese author and entrepreneur says that human consciousness has an effect on the molecular structure of water. He says that positive changes to water crystals can be achieved through prayer or music or by attaching written words to a container of water. Since about two-thirds of the body is made up of water, the same law of nature applies to us. Positive moods (thus well-being) can be achieved through prayer, music or other uplifting activity like spending time with loved ones.

When I was managing the business operations for a big chunk of Cisco's emerging markets (I was responsible for forty countries over several continents), my team and I were greatly affected by the moods of the larger teams working with us. We supported the sales team and acted as its representative in other departments. We had to maintain a sensitive balance, requiring close collaboration between very different characters. Trust and communication were key to our relationship. Among the hundreds of salespeople, there would usually be a few stressed-out types who did not like the corporate rules.

One day I was asked to present on behalf of my team at a meeting. Considering what message to offer, I decided to speak my truth. I kicked off my presentation by pointing to Emoto's discoveries about water, which prove that we have profound effects on each other. I said that our success depends on how we treat each other. Pictures of frozen water crystals were the highlight of my presentation. Water that was prayed over produced amazingly regular and beautiful crystals when frozen. Love and gratitude made them appear perfect in every way. The water to which rude, unloving words were uttered produced very unattractive, even appalling, crystals.

My manager told me that the team might not understand this. I was so sure of my message, however, that I wanted to reach out to those who were ready to grasp it. I went ahead with the presentation, and it was my best ever! I could see the glow on some faces, and knew immediately that I had touched hearts. Many people wanted the name of Emoto's book. I was happy and proud. Most of all, I enjoyed what I had done, which is always the signal that I have followed the right path.

✻✻✻✻✻

FOR AN IMMEDIATE SHIFT in mood, music is a wonderful choice. As we are vibration and music is vibration, uplifting music has a magical and immediate effect on the human body. Music's healing effects are long proven, so why not make use of it?

Music easily enables joy. The Superconscious repeatedly states that the reason we are here is to experience joy. Dolphins are among the most loving beings. They share their joy, communicating through sound, which is like music to our ears. I feel a deep connection to them. In a session where I was the subject, my dolphin guide showed up. He had previously appeared to me in a dream, but now he offered more. He swam with me, taught me about rhythm, and pacing through breath. He showed me his world before finally rejoining his herd. His key message was, "Joy is found within the herd." I share this to emphasize the importance of cultivating friendship. Sharing our experiences with like-minded people is one of the best ways to uplift our spirits and connect to our being.

The simplest way to connect with our being is by doing nothing. When I was working in the corporate world, my spirit guides suggested that I practice the feeling of doing nothing. That was nearly impossible to do back then, since I was chained to my agenda, my checklists, and getting things done. As I slowed down and simplified my life more and more, doing nothing became relatively easy. Still, I have to admit that this is a challenging area for me! I will discuss this subject in chapter 9.

CHAPTER 4

Messages from the Animal Kingdom

Lots of people talk to animals. Not very many listen, though. That's the problem.

—Benjamin Hoff, *The Tao of Pooh*

WHEN AN ANIMAL MAKES an unusual appearance in your life, this means it has a message for you. If you keep an open mind, you will notice the signs from the universe. A sign was not there before, and like the 11:11 phenomenon, it suddenly catches your attention. This is one of the purist forms of synchronicity. And the signals discussed below come directly from Mother Nature. As I share my experiences, this will become clear.

The first messages I received from the animal kingdom—at least the first I was aware of— came through dragonflies. Surely this was no coincidence, since dragonflies represent spiritual enlightenment. A dragonfly's magic is the power of light.

I was still in the corporate world. Following a busy day of conference calls, I was walking in the small garden of my apartment complex. Not knowing what a dragonfly looked like, I found myself gazing at a big, beautiful bug with large wings. She flew ahead of me for quite a while, making sure she was noticed. Then she landed on some leaves, made certain I took a good look at her, and flew over a cement wall.

Researching this extraordinary fly, I stumbled upon a book called *Animal-Speak* in which author Ted Andrews explains animal symbolism in the deepest spiritual way as part of shamanic teaching. He details the laws and energy of nature, asking what animals might symbolize and why they might appear to us. His book has become a wonderful reference for me.

Dragonflies are all about change, and they symbolize a two-year period of colorful transformation. If you see a dragonfly, ask yourself if you are neglecting your emotions or resisting change when you shouldn't. A dragonfly can help you see through your illusions and allow your light to shine forth. This creature brings the brightness of transformation and the wonder of a colorful new vision (Andrews, 340).

For many months after this, I saw dragonflies. Normally, they fly away quickly, but the ones I saw stayed put. They made sure that I saw them and that I got the message.

Seeing them was an eye opener. I had learned to meditate, launching several years of constant change and transformation. As I began to listen to my inner voice, life became more colorful.

During these months, I also started noticing more butterflies, which symbolize transmutation and the dance of joy. They remind us to lighten up and not to take life's events quite so seriously. They awaken a sense of lightness and joy (Andrews, 339). Butterflies help teach us that growth and change do not have to be traumatic, something that resonates deeply with me. In fact, I put butterflies in the cover pictures of the presentations I was giving. I was guided to start a circle and share knowledge and experience with those interested. Sharing experiences triggered awareness shifts in everyone who participated in our meetings throughout that winter.

While my husband and I were attending classes at the Chopra Center to learn to teach meditation, I had an interesting vision. During an evening meditation, I saw a rabbit jump twice, followed by another rabbit, which did the same thing. They came from the right in the vision through pine trees in a snowy forest. It was a beautiful, peaceful scene.

A week later, a German friend sent me an electronic animated Christmas card. When clicked, it produced exactly the same scene—two rabbits jumping, one after the other! Apparently, I had somehow energetically connected to her and her gift a bit ahead of what we experienced as linear time. I felt that the unified field of intelligence was winking at me.

I found that rabbits represent fertility and new life. They are all about movement and making leaps and hops in life. I needed to take advantage of the opportunities that might arise for brief moments. I had to recognize the signs and be ready to act quickly (Andrews, 303).

Amazingly, this vision occurred just a few months before I listened to Dolores Cannon's podcast. To be trained by her just at the time we would be in San Diego was certainly a once-in-a-lifetime opportunity. This was indeed a major leap in my life. And it was a leap of faith, since I knew nothing about Cannon or her work. Still, my heart was clearly pointing in her direction.

✶✶✶✶✶

A FEW YEARS AGO, my husband and I took a week's vacation in Florence, in the hills of Tuscany. I was standing on the upper porch of the hotel, and suddenly something landed on my left hand. It felt large but light. I shook my hand, but it did not go away. It was a big grasshopper. The hotel overlooked a tarmac road and was not in a grassy area. I was surprised at how the insect had suddenly lighted on my hand. It seemed to have come out of nothingness.

Grasshoppers represent uncanny leaps forward. "Take a chance and leap forward" was the message from the universe. "Trust your instincts, your inner voice; what works for others will not necessarily work for you. Then, and only then, will you be able to leap forward into successful ventures." (Andrews, 342)

At this point, I was just starting to practice Quantum Healing Hypnosis Therapy. Coming from an analytical background and having received monthly paychecks, it was quite a shift to work as an independent hypnotherapist. Leaving behind structures, rules, and guidelines required another guide—one beyond thought, a voice within. Since what seemed to work for others did not work for me, I bravely had to discover my own way step by step.

Interestingly, as I began writing this chapter about messages from the animal kingdom, I saw a grasshopper in our house. Since this was the first one we had seen in our three years there, it is obviously sending me a message. What better message could I have from the universe just as I was writing my first book? Follow your own path, trusting your gut feelings!

✼✼✼✼✼

AFTER RETIRING EARLY FROM corporate life, I started to make clay sculptures. My teacher said, "You know the basics now, so please just start playing with the clay and see what comes out. No need to work from a model." And so I did. The mountain of clay got bigger and bigger. Working by instinct without thinking, I said, "It feels like I am making a bird." This sounded strange at the time, but I went on without questioning. Questioning interrupts the flow, something I knew from my oil painting.

Toward the end of the day, I recognized the bird. It was a peacock! I made it unconsciously, somehow picking up the sights I had seen at a hotel in Antalya, Turkey, where we had recently stayed.

I read that peacocks symbolize resurrection and wise vision. The bird's call reminds us to laugh at life. Its feathers have "eyes" on them, so the peacock is associated with mysticism, wisdom, and mythology (Andrews, 181).

Creating this sculpture was a clear message to me that I was moving on to a totally new life, a more mystical one. From then on, I did not need to take life so seriously and could choose to laugh at it.

Amphibians figured in another message. When walking in the forest, I saw dead frogs for three days in a row. If you start running into them, they certainly have a message for you. In this case, the message was that I would be coming into my own creative power through transformation. Since there was a water element, I also needed to examine my emotions. Did I need to dive into fresh creative water? Was I drowning in emotions? (Andrews, 356)

Crows symbolize mysticism. Sometimes when I walk in the forest and approach them, they do not fly away. Then I know that they are signaling me to remember. Crows also symbolize spiritual strength and the secret magic of creation. Intelligent and adaptable, they remind us to look for opportunities to create and to manifest the magic of life every day (Andrews, 130). We just need to notice, stop, and listen to their message.

One incident involving the animal kingdom stands out as the most amazing. We had just signed a contract to move to a log house in the forest. I said to my husband, "Let's have a nice celebration dinner on the Bosporus." We drove to our favorite restaurant and sat near the water. Just as it was getting dark, two dolphins swam toward us, jumping up and down in perfect rhythm. I had never seen dolphins in their natural environment, and I immediately knew that their appearance was not a coincidence. They were celebrating with us. I knew that we had done the right thing in choosing that house.

Dolphins symbolize the power of breath and sound. They can

open the way to new creation and dimensions. They are about rhythm (breathing and swimming). Sound, breath, and water are considered the sources of life. Dolphins are primordial beings. They are masters of breathing and sounding techniques essential to manifestation. We must ask ourselves what our thoughts and words are creating for us. Dolphins suggest that we get out, play, explore, and most of all breathe (Andrews, 266).

Last summer, we started noticing dead bees in my healing room, especially next to my rose quartz crystals. This alarmed us, since bees create life and are sacred. After long research, we asked the Superconscious, which told us that the bees were going to die anyway and chose that place because they found it special. Bees symbolize accomplishing the impossible. They are busy and productive. They remind us that productivity should go hand in hand with enjoying our labors; otherwise we turn into workaholics. The bee reminds us that activities are sweeter and more productive if we take time to savor them. The honeycomb is the symbol of the heart and the sweetness of life found within our hearts (Andrews, 337).

This was a key message for me, since I was busy doing sessions and writing. It had been a very hot and humid summer in Istanbul, so focusing was often a challenge. I clearly needed to switch back to joy and embrace my productive self. After all, I could accomplish the impossible! It was time to remember that as limitless beings, we are cocreators with God.

Last summer, I saw a lizard during a walk. I read that lizards with ruffs around their necks can teach us how to bridge the subconscious and the conscious, or the dreaming and waking states. Lizards with spines signify that the sensitivity of chakras is heightened or about to be. If the life force flows strongly, it will heighten all sensitivities—physical, emotional, mental, psychic, and spiritual. Intuition and psychic perceptions are active or about to be activated more strongly, so we must pay attention. Individuals with a lizard totem should listen to their own intuition over anyone else's. They will feel and see things others will not. Lizards may lose and then regrow their tails. What a lesson in detachment! They can help us to be more detached and to survive. Sometimes it is necessary to separate ourselves from others to do the things we desire. Lizards might show up to help us break from the past (Andrews, 358).

All these messages were timely, coming the day after an interesting hypnotherapy session. The major message from the Superconscious to my client concerned detachment! And I saw the lizard the day after this session. This was jaw-dropping.

Last but not least, I recently ran into a fairly long snake in our garden. In our three years in this place, I had never seen one. In my research, I found that snakes are all about rebirth, transformation, and healing through wisdom. The hypnotherapy sessions are exactly that— healing through connecting with the universal wisdom.

Snakes also symbolize the creative life force. As we develop, we open our minds and bodies to creativity, better health, and new dimensions. Our vision and intuition become more accurate. Snakes' connection to death and rebirth symbolizes the transformation of lead into gold, thus higher wisdom. The trancelike state a snake enters as it sheds its skin is important. During this amazing process, the snake moves between the realms of the living and the dead, crosses over from life to death and back to life. Therefore, when a snake appears to you, expect death and rebirth (a transition) to occur in some area of your life. Are you failing to make changes or are you forcing change too quickly? Just as a snake swallows its prey whole, you will be able to absorb and digest greater amounts of knowledge. A snake's stare is associated with hypnotic qualities; use your eyes to mesmerize and look into the hearts and souls of others (or into your own heart and soul). In short, if a snake comes into your life, you will see changes occurring quickly. You can look for a rebirth into new powers of creativity and wisdom (Andrews, 360).

All this meant a lot to me just as I was writing this book. I needed to digest all the information from the many hypnotherapy sessions and summarize the highlights. More and more awakening souls were knocking on my door for sessions, and I was changing with them throughout our work together.

Chapter 5

A Past Life Never Lies

Why write a book on uncovering past lives? Because the benefits for personal empowerment, healing, and enlightenment are tremendous.

—Ted Andrews, *How to Uncover Your Past Lives*

"I HAVE GONE THROUGH such a transformation that I can only call it a miracle. I will never be the same person again."

This is what I hear from my clients once their awareness is shifted through seeing other realities. More often than not, this happens through seeing their past lives. They glimpse another reality and return to their current lives wiser. Exploring different angles to their lives and souls, most of them instantly eliminate limiting beliefs and fears. Reliving a past life, realizing repeating patterns and lessons, and discovering soul family relationships are all very powerful experiences.

Past lives bring depth and meaning to people's current lives once deciphered with the guidance of a hypnotherapist. They are transformational. Experiencing a past life regression is like opening a door into one's essence, or higher self, especially when it is done with the intention of healing. Returning to past lives out of curiosity is not a good idea. This door is sacred, and one should walk through it in one's own time, at one's own pace, and with a clear intention. A series of synchronistic events will usually take place, and signs like a lantern will light up the stairway to a deeper soul search. A subtle orchestration behind the scenes can be called divine timing. This is the ideal time to step into the unknown, embracing uncertainty with open arms.

The person's higher self, which is part of the unified consciousness, Superconscious, oneness, or oversoul, knows which past life the person needs to experience on the day of the session. This unified field of intelligence knows what the person needs to work and heal at that time, since we are all one. All that is needed is to set clear intentions and allow the healing to take place.

Sometimes people don't see past lives. They stay in their current lives or experience nothingness, the space, the source, extraterrestrial intelligence, or even a glimpse into the future. The experience is very personal and is orchestrated on a need-to-know basis. Their higher selves already know their questions and the roots of their current issues. The higher self knows all there is to know about the eternal soul temporarily residing in a body and is aware of the soul's history. Therefore, wherever people are on their journey and experiencing the wonder of life on earth, their higher selves embrace them with love. Feeling unconditional love during a session brings to mind our oneness. There are no judgments, thus nothing to fear.

What is also amazing is that people are given only the information that they are ready to receive. The path they walk is protected as long as the method is properly applied. This involves an initial relaxation phase, a journey through the client's consciousness, with the therapist as the facilitator, a conversation with the higher self, and finally the crucial bringing out. I call this an all-in-one dive into a person's essence, since the topics that come up are intertwined. Shedding light on those few life lessons and purposes brings the person to a new, elevated state of consciousness.

Many people want scientific proof before they will believe in something and are skeptical of past lives. But research on the facts revealed in sessions would offer countless proofs. Clients have offered details of past lives. Searching the Internet with those details, we have verified the stories, the places, and the times! This confirms the credibility of the information provided during the sessions.

In her many books, my teacher Dolores Cannon details countless cases of past lives and their connection to current lives. Having conducted sessions with thousands of clients, repeatedly recording the same results, and spending vast amounts of time and energy verifying the authenticity of her clients' past lives, she has concluded that her results are genuine and that she had tapped into an incredibly powerful source of information. She has witnessed amazing healing in her patients when they have sorted out past-life issues.

Brian Weiss is the author of the best-selling book *Many Lives, Many Masters*. A graduate of Columbia University and Yale Medical School and chairman emeritus of psychiatry at Mount Sinai Medical Center in Miami, he examines the physical, emotional, and spiritual healing that is possible when one embraces the reality of reincarnation. A traditional psychotherapist, Weiss was astonished and skeptical when a patient began recalling past-life traumas that seemed to hold the key to her recurring nightmares and anxiety attacks. His skepticism faded, however, when she began to channel messages from "the space between lives," which contained remarkable revelations about Weiss's family and his dead son. Using past-life therapy, he helped to cure the patient and embarked on a new, more meaningful phase of his career.

Michael Newton is the founder of The Newton Institute for Life Between Lives Hypnotherapy and the author of *Journey of Souls: Case Studies of Life Between Lives*. He is considered a pioneer in uncovering the mysteries about life after death through the use of Spiritual Regression. He shares his discoveries and beliefs about immortal life in the spirit world, sharing his thousands of cases. He says, "For hidden within are memories of your life as a soul, between incarnations, your life with soul friends and family, planning your future lives on earth."

*****

If you are trapped in patterns of frustration, you need to learn from them. Your conscious mind, disconnected from higher wisdom, cannot fathom the cause of the problem.

Selin, a thirty-year-old client, was unable to stick to any relationship. No one was good enough for her, either as a friend or as a lover. She felt isolated and aloof from everyone. Having a successful career did not fulfill her at all, and she had come to a hypnotherapy session hoping to sort out what was triggering the discomfort felt in close relationships.

The moment she was relaxed in a trance state, Selin saw herself dancing at a wedding in the center of a rural village. A handsome young man stood right across from her, and their eyes were glued to each other. This was not their wedding, but they were to be wed very soon. Their deep love was well known in the community. At that moment, armed men on horses rushed into the village and kidnapped her. In the next scene, she saw herself locked up in a tower by the owner of a castle, a powerful and wealthy man who forced her to marry him. She was helpless and hopeless, wanting to escape but not daring to act. She lived that life imprisoned, apart from the man she loved so dearly. Later on, she had a child, but there was no love in her marriage.

Following these scenes, when Selin allowed her subconscious, or higher self, to come forward, we learned that she was scared to love in her current life, since she felt love might end badly, as it had in her past life. However, because this past life was now released from her subconscious into her conscious mind, she was healed and she could move on. She should not have given up in that past life, and she should have tried to escape from the tower to reunite with her lover. Going forward, she could give men a chance and talk about her issues fearlessly rather than abruptly ending a relationship. Listening to her heart and trusting her feelings were safe! To do this, she would have to allow time alone, read, travel, and write about what she was experiencing. Joining authors' groups would help her get over her loneliness. Above all, Selin would have to make sure she did not give up on herself.

A hypnotherapy session gains magical power by looking at life from an elevated perspective. From that angle, there is no good or bad, right or wrong, just experience. Once a person's consciousness detaches from the body and travels to the most appropriate time and space, the past life becomes the spokesperson, and the person a channel of universal wisdom.

One of my clients, Meltem, an international executive, said, "I recently learned to meditate; however, each time I close my eyes to meditate, I feel extremely uncomfortable and have to reopen my eyes right after I close them. I have slowly realized that my biggest fear, losing my daughter, is somehow triggered when I close my eyes. There is no reason to have such a fear or anxiety, so I have been searching for answers. My mind is not able to sort this issue on its own. I need help."

Meltem became a little emotional, and her eyes were watery.

"I am very mind driven," she continued. "Logic always comes first, and my body-soul-emotions are pretty neglected. Since meditation seemed to be the ultimate form of connecting to one's essence, I took the weekend course and that is when I hit the wall and wasn't able to meditate."

Meltem gently closed her eyes and became deeply relaxed. She immediately saw a beautiful house on a hill, overlooking the sea. The house looked deserted. When I asked her to go back in time and find out what happened in that house, she saw a blonde woman in her thirties living there in isolation. She had married her husband not out of love, but because she was pregnant and he was rich. He was a businessman, traveling all the time, and he was rarely home to spend time with his wife and son. She had never worked and had nothing important in her life other than her son. The boy, also living in isolation, went to school when he turned six. The woman felt very lonely and waited impatiently for him to come home; however, he never returned. We found out through further questions and answers that he had fallen into a nearby river and was never found. The woman was like a vegetable, with no joy, only sadness. She lived with her grief until her passing at eighty years old.

Meltem kept saying that she was making all this up, but the scenes were so vivid and kept appearing so clearly that she continued talking. Sometimes she felt that she was the woman, as if her consciousness and the woman's were merged. At other times, she felt as if she were watching a movie. "At all times, though, I lived it all somehow," she said. "It is very hard to explain. It is a totally experiential process."

By that point, Meltem was very emotional, shedding tears. This was quite a journey; she seemed to be experiencing a simultaneous life. It was all so real. Quantum physicists say that time does not exist and that all realities are happening now. "Well, I somehow felt this myself," she said.

As the past life most relevant to her current life (and life lessons) was laid out, we needed to talk to her subconscious, her higher self. As Meltem allowed this wise part of her to come forward, she said that she had chosen the past life to learn to withstand pain and grief. Her current life was actually a gift, since she had suffered so much in that long and sad past life. If she would be more flexible and stop thinking negatively, her husband and daughter would be happier and healthier. She should let go, not be so uptight, and trust the divine. Meltem also said that she was always told what she needed to know and that she should regularly stop and listen. She could talk to the divine directly and ask whatever she needed to know, getting answers in her sleep state.

After she emerged from the trance state and we were talking about her experience, Meltem said that she clearly felt the woman say, "Next time, I will do it differently. I will not marry someone I do not love. I will not live in such isolation. I will have a life outside of raising my child and perhaps get a job. Also, I will not blame my husband, but will take responsibility for my life and my family's life." Her past life was indeed a tough and unhappy life.

"What is truly amazing," said Meltem, "is that this is my voice, but these are words I would not normally use, appearing in sentences that I would not usually choose. I would not believe all this if I did not listen to the recording of the session. My voice turned very deep, too. It was as if my wiser part were speaking, looking at my life from an entirely new perspective."

Following this session, Meltem was able to meditate, leaving the fear behind.

I would like to share some words from Dolores Cannon. She is always encouraging us to leave fear behind and continue practicing Quantum Healing Hypnosis. I love her direct approach and pragmatism:

"The Inquisition was over ages ago. Been there, done that. The majority of us have been there also on both sides as the accused and the accuser. So it's now time to learn from it and move on and leave the fear behind. This is a beautiful work, and you can perform miracles by using it positively and not allowing fear to hold you back from what you can accomplish. When you cling to fear, you won't be working with 'them' (the Superconscious), the highest creative power there is. This therapy is so needed in this important time, so let's all get back to work and not be sidetracked."

Chapter 6

Self-Love

Through Love all that is bitter will be sweet.
Through Love all that is copper will be gold.
Through Love all dregs will turn to purest wine.
Through Love all pain will turn to medicine.
Through Love the dead will all become alive.
Through Love the king will turn into a slave!

—Rumi

"You are here only to experience life and to love. Your first and foremost responsibility is to yourself."

It was not the first time that my potential client, Tuba, had heard this, but she could not digest it—at least not yet. A high-level executive at a prominent company, she was the mother of two girls. She and her husband had grown apart long ago and had decided to go their own ways. For more than a year, Tuba had been a single mom, juggling her duties. Life did not seem to work for her, and she was chronically unhappy. She could not remember a happy place or a happy thought. Life was a bitter joke, almost a misery, and a heavy burden to carry.

Looking back, she thought she had always done the right things at the right time with the right people. Her education had gone smoothly, and she was successful. She had a reputation for being honest, trustworthy, and responsible—maybe too responsible. She frequently volunteered without a second thought, shared her energy sparingly, helped others first, and put herself second.

She did not understand how self-love could help her with her mountain of challenges. Her girls wanted her undivided attention, her managers' demands were too much to take, and her ex-husband had moved on to another life. She felt lonely, hopeless, drained. She needed a miracle.

Tuba was quite skeptical about spirituality. She preferred books on business and competition. At least those helped her with her challenges at work. She also read about raising children and about relationships, which seemed to help her tackle her day-to-day life more effectively. After all, she needed to be superproductive to survive. Even though she had a good nanny to take care of her daughters, she still had lots to manage.

In this nonjudgmental space, she was now hearing about how easy changing one's life could be. This was music to Tuba's ears, since she was ready to do whatever it took to shift and move on. If only there were a user's manual to consult! Her quick, analytical mind would easily absorb the information and apply it to her life. This was one of her key strengths. She could learn so very quickly. Even her most demanding bosses had said, "You are like a sponge. You learn and apply at the speed of light." She was proud of this, since it made life bearable in her fast-paced world.

As our conversation progressed, Tuba often appeared to be entering a different reality, one beyond the rat race in which she was trapped. I said, "Once you choose the path of opening your heart, life will be a joyful journey. And this is surprisingly easy to do."

I suggested that Tuba make a list of things she enjoyed doing and another list of things she would rather not do. She said there was a great deal she would prefer not to do, but she had to think hard to remember what gave her joy. The time spent with her girls, and the few happy memories from the early years of her marriage, immediately came to mind. Thinking further back, she smiled and said that she remembered her first true love in high school. All of that was history now, and she said that she felt she was in a rut.

"To listen to your inner voice and find out who you really are, you need to calm down your mind chatter," I said. "As I learned at the Chopra Center University, research shows that on average, every human being has sixty to eighty thousand thoughts a day. This is inevitable and is pretty draining, confusing, and overwhelming. An executive like you would be especially prone to having an overactive mind. Is that the case?"

Tuba mentioned the many nights when she would wake up at three or four o'clock with flashes about tasks to be done by the nanny, an activity to delegate at work, or yet another conflict she needed to sort out with her ex-husband. She could not relax enough to have a quality sleep. Even when she pampered herself at a spa or treated herself to a long weekend away from it all, her head was a jungle of thoughts. Sleeping longer hours over the weekend did not seem to help either. She still woke up heavy and stiff as a rock.

"I am aware that I need to change something," she said, "but I'm not sure what it is or how."

For as long as she could remember, Tuba had not been ambitious. Her natural qualities had brought her to where she was. She had the rare gift of active listening, which meant that whatever she concentrated on she would conquer. She saw the big picture and went to the heart of the matter in no time. "But why can't I do this in my emotional life?" she asked.

"Working at mind level is a confined way of looking at the miracle of life," I explained. "There is so much more to discover if one delves into the vast consciousness, which is part of the source. In a nutshell, we can call this discovering the interconnectedness of existence. A holistic approach is the ultimate path; physical, mental, spiritual, and emotional aspects are all equally important.

"It all goes back to self-love, and the key to that is self-acceptance through increased awareness. It is no coincidence that your soul has chosen to incarnate into this body and into this life scenario. Have you ever wondered what you are here to experience and learn?

"It is great that you are searching for answers rather than continuing to sweat rowing your boat upstream. There is always a downstream, an effortless way to experience life, and it takes only the blink of an eye to shift tracks. The key is to decide to change tracks, to intend to change and transform. The universe collaborates big time when you take even a baby step in that direction."

At that moment, Tuba said that she suddenly felt her heart beat like never before. It was as if time had frozen and she was floating above the clouds, weightless, carefree, hopeful, joyful.

What I described was a flow that she always intuitively knew to be possible. Since her first weeks in corporate life, she had observed that the core work did not take long. A three-day workweek would be enough to run the business. The remaining time spent at work involved unproductive meetings, communication challenges, and big egos. Keeping up appearances was a major part of the game, too. Looking busy mattered.

Tuba's intent to transform was strong, and she was curious to hear what her baby steps could be. I noted that transformation was much more definitive than change. You could always revert to the old ways if you fell into the same rut. But once you were transformed, there would be no going back. "The element of fire symbolizes transformation," I said. "And the best time to connect with the transformational energies of nature is during the full moon through the full moon ritual. The moon represents femininity. Because of this, the lunar cycle is especially important to us women. Why not use these energies to clear and uplift your life?"

I do this quick ritual every month on the day of the full moon, and I have been able to shift so much in my life with this little habit. And it is effortless. I write down whatever I do not want in my life anymore and then burn that piece of paper, throwing the ashes into the sea. I regularly experience this transformational process. I would not miss a full moon! It is important that I thank all those issues and then burn the paper. All events and experiences are building blocks of our lives. As we move on and expand our consciousness, we simply drop the parts we no longer need. No experience is ever wasted. All are valuable even if they may be painful at the time.

"Accepting yourself unconditionally nourishes self-love," I said. Then I shared the highlights of a previous session with a lady in her mid forties. She was always helping those in need, mostly her large extended family. She was burned out and wanted to eliminate the pressure of helping so many people all the time. The Superconscious explained that she was the one restricting and pushing herself. She always did all she possibly could, and it was time to experience peace. If she valued herself, everyone would! Once she ended the interdependence between her and all those she was helping, they would also start to shift their awareness. The key for her was surrendering without thinking too much about details. She needed to remember that whatever would happen would happen. Sometimes it is best to keep silent and observe others calmly. As in many sessions with other clients, the Superconscious recommended that she listen to her inner voice and learn to meditate. Writing poems and painting would also be very beneficial. In this way, she would shift her mind from tasks and express her creativity.

Hearing all of this, Tuba left our meeting feeling hopeful and lighter in spirit. She said she felt more equipped for life. Looking into one's essence is always important, as this reveals the simple steps required to shift one's awareness and thus one's life. This is a lifelong venture.

CHAPTER 7

Attitude of Gratitude

The mystic dances in the sun,
hearing music others don't.
"Insanity," they say, those others.
If so, it's a very gentle,
nourishing sort.

—Rumi

TUBA WAS INTRIGUED BY the alternate realities people seemed to experience and was certainly willing to discover further. I explained that there are three easy ways to communicate with our subconscious: dreams, meditation, and hypnotherapy. Through dreams, we can get an endless number of messages from our essences. We must write these messages down immediately after waking up, since dreams fade away like vapor. In dreams, the subconscious most often uses symbolism to get its messages across to the conscious mind. When we record these, we bring key information from the subconscious mind to the conscious mind, which has an immediate healing effect on the soul. Seeing the patterns and asking ourselves what the symbols mean help us to become more aware. I will further explore dreams in chapter 14.

Meditation is another way of connecting to the subconscious mind. Through meditation, we can effortlessly listen to our essences and to the universe itself and hear messages from the field of pure potentiality, which is infinite intelligence. In his lectures,

Chopra says, "When we pray, we talk to God. When we meditate, God talks to us." This calm state is a balm for our being.

Finally, through hypnotherapy, it is possible to connect directly to the universal wisdom, with one major bonus: the therapist can have a Q&A with the client's higher self based on the person's intentions and healing needs. Unlike the other two methods, this one offers guidance and support from a therapist, ensuring that the right questions are asked and that the appropriate healing on all levels is requested. These levels include physical, mental, spiritual, and emotional.

All this sounded magical, and Tuba listened attentively.

I shared a session I had with Ceyda, a fifty-year-old doctor, who had come to achieve inner peace, find meaning and joy in life, and connect with her feelings. She was overly judgmental of herself and of her marriage, which had recently ended after twenty-plus years.

As the session began, I offered my usual analogy, saying that a hypnotherapy session frees anything that must be released from the system, just like the steam coming out of a pressure cooker. Ceyda interrupted me and said, "Oh, Esra, I dreamed of a pressure cooker last night!"

This is pretty common; the subconscious mind speeds up communication with the client, starting from the moment the person decides to have a session. Therefore I always recommend that clients keep a dream journal until they see me. I also ask them to take notes on unusual events that happen in their lives, such as messages from the animal kingdom.

In the dream, Ceyda opened the pressure cooker before it had cooled off. She feared that it might explode, but nothing happened. What a wonderful message! The dream told Ceyda that all was well, that she could allow her conscious mind to step aside, and that she should stop controlling and analyzing. In this way, Ceyda was able to get all the answers she needed from her higher self and received the healing she needed, all within the divine order.

During this session, music, dancing, and color frequently came up as gentle cures and ways to embrace joy. Ceyda was advised to love the easy path, be happy with small steps, and stop expecting too much from herself. To find inner peace, she was told to help others, perhaps teach. Self-love would come from surrendering, choosing to stay in the moment, feeling gratitude, and being patient. "Do not think too much, but flow like water," was the wise advice given to her. She was told to shift to an attitude of gratitude and be happy simply because she was alive. The key was to find joy by choosing whatever made her feel good. Joy and self-confidence would eventually take her to the work that would satisfy her. She was also advised to regularly connect with her inner wisdom through meditation.

Ceyda had learned to meditate about five months earlier, but was not practicing it regularly. She had let it slip and was feeling uncomfortable about this, since she had experienced the amazing positive effects of meditation. During our talk after the session, I explained that connecting to one's essence twice a day is exponentially more effective than doing this only once a day. It is very helpful to meditate in the morning before starting your day, since this clears away the activities of the mind during the night. Similarly, meditating after a busy day clears the mind again, preparing you for a nourishing sleep.

✹✹✹✹✹

THE MOST COMMON MESSAGE from the universal field of intelligence is that we should help others, share our experiences with them, and live joyful lives with an attitude of gratitude. This reflects my view of life. I have always felt that the more I shared with others the more colorful my life became. This attitude has brought richness to my life and to the lives of those I have helped. This was how I optimized the synergy in my workplace during my corporate life. I saw that one plus one was making three when all team members shared in abundance with clear, common goals in mind. Positive energies gave birth to more positive energies, having a snowball effect.

Such synergy is possible in every area of life and functions outside of time and space. The crucial point is that everyone involved uses the power of attention and intention in a focused way. Research carried out by many prestigious institutions worldwide clearly shows the tremendous power of meditation. Meditators sitting in simple silence, with focused attention and intention, change the consciousness of masses.

I have repeatedly observed that the feeling of gratitude quickly and magically shifts our vibration to a higher level. Starting from this feeling, it takes much less effort to see the positivity that surrounds us. During one of my sessions, my client Asuman said that she lacked belief and trust, doubted God, and thought that abundance and power were "not enough." She felt very tired and said that living her life required too much effort. This left her in a controlling and fearful state.

During the trance state, she was shown two past lives. In the first one, she was a thirty-year-old man, dressed like a legionnaire, carrying a spear, and living in a tent. Later on, she said that he was a paid soldier. He had no home, no family, and no purpose. On an important day, he was celebrating a victory, eating and drinking with others; however, he felt the victory was meaningless. When he was much older, he died in battle, wounded in the gut in the desert, and vultures ate his remains. He suffered no pain, feeling that his body was meaningless. He was happy to die, since there was no love in his life. In fact, there was no one else of importance to him. His whole life was about fighting.

Asuman then saw a second past life. This time she was a man in his twenties, a beggar in ragged clothes. When he was older, he was killed on the street by people who ridiculed and kicked him. When he died, they carried him away and cleaned the street. As he left his body, he felt no shame over begging and realized that this was the only thing he could do to survive. He made a firm decision that never again would he feel belittled. "I am very valuable," he said. "We all are valuable under any and all circumstances. I will show everyone how valuable I am."

Following these scenes, I called forth Asuman's higher self, who said that she should feel gratitude for her current life. She should value it, standing strong and firm in her pride. She had been given so much: a family and lots of love. This was a valuable life. She was advised to welcome love, since she got none in her past lives. To have an effortless life, her higher self said, she should often stop and watch; there was nothing to fear. Everything is love, and she needed to see the love surrounding her and her family. The only absolute truth is love.

Chapter 8

Trusting Your Inner Voice

*To obey no other external command, only the [inner] voice, to
be prepared—that was good, that was necessary.
Nothing else was necessary.*

—Hermann Hesse, *Siddhartha*, 39

ONCE WE INTEND TO change, our inner voices immediately become more vocal. Moreover, just like building muscles with exercise, the more we listen to this wise voice, the stronger it gets. That is because we are honoring and appreciating it. A deep, loving relationship is blooming.

The initial step is to start hearing the voice within. I have already mentioned some of the ways to hear it, such as being in nature or meditating. In such relaxing moments, we have a much higher chance of allowing the voice to emerge.

Another wonderful way to hear your inner voice is through inspirational writing. This begins with attunement of the ego to an ideal, and the writing that follows is an expression of that experience. Inspirational writing, unlike the automatic kind, goes hand in hand with spiritual development. Automatic writing can channel any message from the universal intelligence that is lingering over you, while inspirational writing, beginning with an ideal, channels the higher self. After some meditation, a good way to start is to write out your ideal in a word or a phrase. You may write your ideal over and over for a while. Then, when something comes to mind, write. It's very important to let go of self-consciousness and judgment and simply write. A playful attitude can be helpful. Focus your attention more on staying in the spirit of your ideal and less on what you are writing. Pay attention to staying with the feeling, and write what comes naturally.

I would like to briefly mention Edgar Cayce, who has been called the sleeping prophet, the father of holistic medicine, and the most documented psychic of the twentieth century. For more than forty years, Cayce gave psychic readings to thousands of seekers while in an unconscious state, diagnosing illnesses, revealing past lives, and making prophecies. He was a legendary healer.

The process above is further detailed in Henry Reed's book called *Edgar Cayce on Channeling Your Higher Self (Reed, Chapter 6)*.

✷✷✷✷✷

I LOVE DOING INSPIRATIONAL writing after my meditation practice. I light a candle, which puts me in a relaxed state and brings me to the present moment. I turn on my computer, write down a topic I have in mind, and ask, *What do I need to know now?*

After asking, I wait with eyes closed for a few minutes, and then words are whispered in my ear or visions appear before me. Without questioning or judging any of this, I write it down nonstop. I stay with the feeling and write what flows through my consciousness. I write until there is no more to write; I know this, since the flow stops.

Staying totally detached from the outcome is key to enjoying the process. As in a hypnotherapy session, whatever one needs to experience is right there and is exactly what will surface. Trust it, and it works like magic.

You might prefer to do this exercise with pen and paper. It is your call. Whatever feels comfortable is probably the right method for you. If nothing comes on one day, try on another. We change every day, so do not give up!

Initially when I sat down and did this exercise, I helped myself by getting the space and intention clear. I would write at the top of the page: "I am attuning to my higher self to receive the best guidance! My intention is necessary to engage my intuition; so my intention today is___"

Sometimes I would have a specific topic in mind and ask, *What is my mission? What do I need to do to achieve this?* or *What is your message to me today? How can I help and serve others?*

Some months after I started this practice, I asked, *Is there anything I need to know, I need to do, or any place I need to go for the highest good?*

The answer helped launch my blog writings, which are small poems from my heart. What I very clearly heard was:

There is nothing to know except knowing yourself.

There is nothing to do; all deeds are temporary.

There is nowhere to go; you are where your consciousness is. You can go wherever you want the moment you want.

Just follow the signs; this is enough. Flow. Just flow.

When you remember that time does not exist, you realize that there is only the present moment. This is the secret—to live each moment abundantly to your heart's content. Period.

You can imagine how deeply I was moved by this. These were wise words. It was as if someone else was speaking through me or through my consciousness. Looking back, I cannot help recalling what Deepak Chopra often tells his audiences: "Just watch your thoughts. Who is thinking those thoughts?" At this moment one can only surrender to the big force, the master organizer, the oneness. Buddha, Rumi, and Jesus were those luminous ones who transcended the illusion of the world and worked to teach this truth to others. They saw behind the veil and felt one with everything. They fully embraced unity consciousness.

Cayce said, "Pray hard, as if everything depended on God, but work hard, as if everything depended on you." (Reed, Chapter 10) So keep writing! He said that it is most important to test the guidance received by putting it into action. Then you will receive more guidance. Evaluate guidance from a practical perspective. Is it constructive? Workable? Relevant? And most important, is it consistent with your ideal? If not, disregard it or do more soul searching to ensure that you have chosen the right ideal for you. Always remember that you must be willing to act on the guidance you receive. That is the primary way of learning in life. Author Henry Reed paraphrases Cayce, "Don't ask the question if you're not ready to take responsibility for the answer. Knowledge not applied [is] much more costly than the bliss of ignorance." (Reed, Chapter 10)

As we incorporate service to others into our lives, we are inspired to fully use our abilities. We receive what we give. Expressing ourselves through service is our ultimate purpose. To channel the higher self ultimately involves being ourselves. This naturally happens as the distance between our potential and our actuality grows smaller, and our self-acceptance grows with our self-esteem.

✶✶✶✶✶

I would like to share the highlights of a session at which the message repeatedly concerned trust. My client Gonca was a bright lady in her fifties. She easily returned to a past life where she saw herself as a young man. He and his younger brother were forced to flee when their village was burned down. They were caught and sent to separate work camps as prisoners of war. After years of working in the fields, he met a girl and married her. His wife got pregnant, but the baby was stillborn. This tragedy reminded him of his previous big loss, and he left his wife to look for his brother. After a long search, he found his brother's grave. He felt guilty that he could not protect him. He returned to his wife, but could not be happy anymore. He could not love his wife anymore, and she died from the pain. After this tragedy, the man lived and died alone.

I asked the man's life lessons.

G: This life was for experiencing true love, like he had for his brother and his wife. Also, he had to overcome pain, to let people go, and not be attached. He needed to allow others to go their way. The pain for his brother killed his wife. He was overwhelmed by guilt, but the lesson was the acceptance of both deaths—of his brother and also of the baby.

When Gonca allowed her higher self to emerge, I asked why this life was shown to her.

G: To show her the truth and the meaning of her experience. She experienced a big pain due to her brother, wife, and son. The end of pain is happiness … She does not enjoy life anymore because of her worries and pain. She should remember that her happiness may help others. She needs to be flexible toward life. Acceptance, with no wish to change things, is the lesson. She needs to trust more.

E: What are some tips you can give her?

G: She should meditate, relax, and increase her self-esteem.

E: How can she increase her self-esteem?

G: By realizing a part of herself that has not been realized yet.

E: How?

G: Through creativity, a part she has denied. Maybe writing or photography. She should trust herself!

E: How about her worries concerning abundance and money?

G: She needs to trust that all is well.

E: Why did she choose her family?

G: For a real challenge in the way of trusting.

E: Why did she marry her husband?

G: Together, they needed to learn true love.

E: What is the definition of true love?

G: To trust the other person, give confidence, help, and support through your own life and the other person's life, working together.

E: Anything she needs to know about her parents?

G: She should send them light and be more forgiving because they did their best.

E: Any last messages for her?

G: Never despair. Remember the light. She should take care of herself, trust, apply more discipline in her life around use of time, and increase her awareness.

On another occasion, I had a session with Ahmet, a gentleman in his forties. He had taken a break from corporate life and wanted to learn his life purpose, his mission. Although he saw many scenes and could easily visualize, he was not shown a past life.

When he was relaxed, I called forth his higher self, who said that he was not shown past lives because "he belongs to the future." He was not yet ready to hear his life purpose. The most important message for him was to trust. "He will not have any abundance issues; did he ever have any? He is always protected. He has overcome the barriers we have given him; he should not give up because of the smaller ones to come."

Ahmet wanted insight about bringing up his young daughter, and the answer was that his daughter had chosen him and his wife, and that she was a responsible kid. He was told simply to give her endless love and not try to shape her in any way.

Overall, he was advised to continue to love everyone, not to doubt, and to keep listening to his inner voice.

Chapter 9

Your Body Speaks to You

Both thought and the senses were fine things, behind both of them lay hidden the last meaning; it was worthwhile listening to them both, to play with both, neither to despise nor overrate either of them, but to listen intently to both voices.

—Hermann Hesse, *Siddhartha, 39.*

ONE LITTLE EXERCISE I do with clients before a session is a body scan. I ask them to close their eyes, bring their awareness to their bodies, and see if they feel tension anywhere. This exercise quickly takes them from the mind to the body. It takes them away from doing and thinking to feeling. Their brain waves drop from the beta state (the waking state, when their eyes are open) to the alpha state (the meditative, light trance state). With deep breaths, they start to relax. Now the inner voice has an opportunity to express itself. The body is turned into a barometer, clearly reporting where there is tension.

Even if you do not have time to go deep within, just closing your eyes for a few minutes, breathing deeply, and asking your body for a message is very powerful because this brings you to present-moment awareness. In his timeless classic, *The Seven Spiritual Laws of Success,* Deepak Chopra quotes the immortal guiding words of the Zen sage Lao Tzu, who said, "An integral being knows without going, sees without looking, and accomplishes without doing." (Chopra, 53) In our goal-oriented society where everything is about the effort to achieve, it seems contradictory that we could accomplish our objectives with less effort. But that is the power of the present moment, pregnant with possibilities, infinite in its creativity, whole, perfect, pure, and able to flow in any direction.

Chopra once explained to us in class that the basic human form is the doing state. If we choose to evolve, we experience the thinking state. Instead of reacting to events, we make conscious choices based on our thoughts. Although this is a more advanced state, it is not a holistic approach, since it is disconnected from the heart, which quietly whispers our inner voice. We enter the feeling state when we reach this more connected level. We pay attention to our emotions and honor them. When deciding to take a step, we factor in what our gut says. Beyond this is the being state. We are human beings, and we are here to experience life, exercising our free will as we choose.

In the corporate world, I kept telling anyone who cared to listen, "To see what is happening around you, you first need to slow down or even stop. Think of it this way. How much can you see when you are running nonstop? Not as much as at your walking pace, right? Just slowing down is a wonderful start. Once you slow down, you will naturally relax and open the doors to the possibility of going beyond the structure of the mind."

I chose this path, walking from doing toward being. And I believe this path is how we can remember who we are and recognize the gem within.

Ask yourself this, *"If not now, when?"* This will help you to pursue without delay what is dear to your heart.

When I had my illness, this was the question I constantly posed. My body had clearly told me it was not going to survive where I had placed it. I had a decision to make. I chose to change my direction big time.

I did all the things that I enjoyed doing and did not even

consider the ones I did not enjoy. I took the same approach with people around me. I did not spend time with anyone I was not totally comfortable with. It is easy to recognize discomfort, since your heart is squeezed and your energy is drained. You want to leave as soon as possible!

Your body is the vehicle through which the energetic plane speaks to you. If you listen to it, you are communicating with the unseen energetic world. Time freezes, and you are in the present moment.

The most profound way your body speaks to you is through your skin. Each time I talk about the moon rituals, the power of intention, or anything close to my heart, I get goose bumps. This happens most often in sessions or when I speak to clients over the phone. This is a clear sign from the universe that I am on my path. Each time I speak my truth or hear truth, I have goose bumps. What a wise signaling mechanism the body offers!

It is important to note that goose bumps happen without our effort or intervention. It is not a thinking process, but a feeling process.

Louise Hay's marvelous book *You Can Heal Your Life* is a great guide to signs from the body. You can consult a list and find out the possible causes of any symptom you are experiencing. Repeating the affirmation suggested brings miraculous recoveries. Although these general guidelines are helpful, the message from the higher self usually provides deeper, more personalized reasons and remedies. That is the power of the Superconscious!

I once worked with Eda, a woman in her late thirties, who had a serious autoimmune disease. She said that she felt she never belonged here on earth. She could not get used to being in her body. When in trance state, her higher self said that she was incarnated for the first time, directly from the source, and would not return to earth. She should have been alone in this life, so each time she fell in love or thought of getting married or having kids, her illness kicked in. She had more attacks with every new event not on her life path. She is married now and has a baby daughter, who is directly from the source as well. The daughter came to increase Eda's awareness. Eda had no karma but created some by having her child. She needs to return to the source, but she must first raise her daughter. It is amazing that she manifests everything and so quickly. She gave many examples. Over the years, doctors put all kinds of labels on her, including dissociative personality (claiming she was three people in one) and schizophrenia.

During the session, she was shown two past lives. The first was one of her mother's past lives and the second her ex-boyfriend's. Both past lives were in Japan, where there are very high, special energies. I was not surprised to hear this, since I adored the serenity I experienced in Japan, especially in Kyoto.

I asked if she was one of the volunteers (as explained in Dolores Cannon's wonderful book *The Three Waves of Volunteers and the New Earth*) and the answer was, "If she wants to be, yes." She was an adventurer, so she wanted to experience life on earth under the toughest circumstances. Her father left her mother, Eda, and her younger sister when she was only two and a half years old. She met him again when she was twenty-five, and they talked for only fifteen minutes. Afterward, she put him out of her thoughts. Her mother had been having panic attacks as far back as Eda could remember.

We were told that Eda would recover from her illness and be able to run again, something she loves, since this is when she feels closest to "them."

This case is an outstanding one in which the body talked to my client. The body wanted her to remember why she was here, but she did not listen. This is typical. The Superconscious often says, "We told her, but she did not listen."

My client immediately felt better. She reported to me that she could move with greater ease right after the session and during the days that followed. She felt wonderful as she remembered and experienced her limitless being.

*****

I would like to mention a few repeated suggestions from the Superconscious regarding good health:

Oxygen: regularly spend time in clean air.

Hydration: drink clean water well before you are thirsty.

Exercise: even very light exercise keeps the body and the cells active and healthy.

Light diet: eat (mostly raw) vegetables, cut down on red meat, chicken, and even fish.

Removal of toxins: cleanse your systems through healthy detoxification programs.

Reduction of stress: relax and rest your mind and body regularly, meditate, and do yoga.

Chapter 10

Creating with Colors

Love was a feeling completely bound up with color, like thousands of rainbows superimposed one on top of the other.

—Paulo Coelho

I HAVE BEEN FASCINATED with colors all my life. Starting with painting and pottery in my early school days, I loved playing with colors, especially vibrant ones. Later on, I reflected this passion in my clothing choices. Rather than hiding behind dark colors, I chose lighter, livelier colors. During that time, I started reading about colors and color healing.

I was attracted to different colors depending on my mood. I would be drawn to wear an orange sweater and realize afterward that I needed to cheer up that day. Orange represents joy. For my sessions, I am almost always drawn to wear blue, the color of healing (as you will read in the session highlights below). Sometimes, I feel I need to wear red, and at other times, I am drawn to everything purple.

Color is a wonderful way to express emotions. I experience this in my oil painting. Choosing colors without thinking is a wonderful way to stay present.

Mandala painting is great for playing with color and turning within. Whatever is hidden in you finds a way to speak. *Mandala* is a Sanskrit word meaning "circle." In this case, the circle refers to the symbol for all that is, especially all that can be, or creation's complete potential, the unmanifest.

Above all, though, the color turquoise deserves a special place in this chapter.

Ever since I opened my heart, I have loved the colors blue and green. As I looked into the energy and spiritual meaning behind each color, I found that turquoise is blue plus green with a hint of yellow. It has been my favorite color for many years. The word essentially means "Turkish." I wanted to include the Turkish culture in this work, and what could be better than putting the country in the title? It resonated with what I wanted to share. Turquoise is a widely used color in traditional Turkish art. Tiles, ceramics, and miniatures all use this color extensively. In fact, we call turquoise Turkish blue.

Turquoise is a bluish tone of green. The color is based on the gem turquoise. In the Old and New Worlds, this gemstone has been esteemed for thousands of years as a holy stone, a talisman bringing good fortune.

During my research, I learned that the word *turquoise* came from the French word for *Turkish* (*Turquois*) and was first used around the sixteenth century. This gemstone adorned places of worship in Turkey, and turquoise was traded in Turkish bazaars and eventually brought to Europe through Turkey (then part of the Ottoman Empire) along with other Silk Road novelties by merchants and travelers. Turquoise jewelry is exceptional in that no two pieces have the same pattern.

Turquoise is a bridging color. It represents the higher heart, making contact with oneself, communication of the heart, unconditional love, self-respect, respect for all life, and taking individual responsibility. The blue in turquoise symbolizes the heavens, and green symbolizes the earth.

Turquoise stones have impressive metaphysical properties and are powerful healing stones that filter the fifth element, ether, into the etheric body. The natural energy of these stones helps us communicate with truth, and their unique vibration resonates with truth's energy. They are strong stones of spiritual attunement and are very effective in aiding creative communication.

As a master healer, turquoise promotes love, kindness, and understanding. It activates the heart (green) and throat (blue) chakras, aids meditation and peace of mind, and purifies thought and behavior patterns. The unusual energy produced within the throat chakra helps us to speak with truth, wisdom, and forthrightness. It stimulates the thymus center (gland), or higher heart chakra. This chakra is said to have been only recently awakened by cosmic time, and it helps us to be more compassionate and to forgive others who do not act compassionately. This strong compassionate vibration resonates out, affecting all areas of the body. This stone's energy works in a diverse range of ways within different chakras and has a strong ability to aid us in living life with integrity and truth. Turquoise stones may be helpful if one wants to work in psychic employment, since they enhance effectiveness in communicating what comes through the spirit in day-to-day physical life.

Turquoise strengthens the body's meridians and subtle energy fields, enhancing communication between the physical and spiritual worlds. The distinct vibration of these stones resonates within the throat and third-eye chakras, allowing one to access past-life knowledge when meditating. Placed on the third eye, a turquoise stone supports intuition and meditation. On the throat chakra, it releases old vows and inhibitions if appropriate and allows the soul to express itself once more. The green in turquoise grounds psychic seeing in the heart, and then clear seeing (blue) can result. It may also help manifest clairaudient and clairvoyant abilities.

✣✣✣✣✣

Other connections resonate with me, and explaining them requires brief information about the Turkish world.

The turquoise gemstone is known as *firuze* in the Eastern world. The color has been employed extensively in the decorative tiles adorning Turkish places of worship and homes for hundreds of years, beginning with the Seljuk Turks. It is also associated with the color of the Mediterranean Sea on the southern Turkish coast.

The healing powers of turquoise were well known in the Turkish world. Many mosques and ancient hospitals in Turkey and the Turkish-origin ex-Soviet republics used this powerful color. As medical historians note, the Turkish world, especially in medieval times, was highly advanced in the healing arts, especially in treating psychiatric illnesses. Healers, whose fame spread beyond the Turkish world, made extensive use of music, color, herbs, and stones.

When Westerners hear the word *Turkish*, they usually associate it with the geographical land of the modern Republic of Turkey of today, which bridges the European and Asian continents. This area is also known as Asia Minor, or Anatolia. But the Turkish World is a phenomenon beyond the geographical borders of this land. It has its roots in an area far from the Turkey of today in the Central Asian Republics. These countries range from Azerbaijan (closest to Turkey) all the way to Kazakhstan.

The ancient spiritual wisdom embedded in the Turkish culture has had a deep influence and been a great help in my spiritual healing and transformation. I was born and raised in Turkey, and the collective consciousness of Turkish culture is naturally a big part of my healing journey. My family originally came from Konya in central Turkey, the land where the thirteenth-century mystic Rumi lived from his teens until his death.

Rumi was born in the Afghan province of Balkh, which is now

Tajikistan. He migrated to the city of Konya during the Mogul invasions. Rumi's philosophy and poetry are all about unity, oneness, and love. This is what the world needs most urgently.

✵✵✵✵✵

Before detailing a session related to colors, I would like to share another synchronicity I had with Kala Ambrose.

One evening, I watched one of her videos. The topic, color scope, was one of my favorites. Ambrose was talking to Elizabeth Harper about colors they had picked earlier and had meditated on. To my amazement, their first choice was turquoise!

"Turquoise is the color of the new age," they said. "It connects to networking, media, and reaching out there to something new. Turquoise green is reconnecting to heart, linking overseas with networking. Turquoise blue is about marketing, media, new opportunities, and about opening a new door to what your heart wants. Turquoise is the healing color. It is more spiritual healing than physical healing. It keeps us centered."

All of this was like a miracle, so timely and such a confirmation of my intuition!

I had just decided to write about my work, and the book was to be published and marketed worldwide by a US printing house. It included aspects of the new age, and most important, highlights of Quantum Healing Hypnosis from my sessions. My hope was that it would connect us and bring us closer to unity through change and transformation. The importance of being heart centered and heart driven was the book's key theme. Finally, spiritual healing is what I do through hypnotherapy, and this healing manifests itself into the physical at the most appropriate time.

✣✣✣✣✣

Here is a session that I have chosen to share in conversation form, since that expresses the messages better. It flows in its own logic.

My client, Tracey, was a lady in her fifties. Immediately after entering a trance state, she saw an old man leading her to a churchlike school. She was a young man being educated there. I questioned what she was doing.

T: I understand the vibrations of blue. I am able to use it, constructing and moving within it.

E: What did you learn about the vibrations of blue that you are using now and are competent in?

T: I learned to walk the vibration, to move within the vibration. This vibration carries a feeling. Although very loving, it has specific healing qualities. You step into this vibration. You think yourself there. It is not physically within you, but you are part of it; the vibration is part of you. It's not solid, but more like stepping into a cloud. I'm now competent with it. At first, I could not grasp it because my mind was in the way.

E: Were there others with you at his school?

T: There were around ten of us. We each worked with different colors. Mine was sky blue. Next to me was orange. There were two greens. There was a light green and a darker, more forest green, which felt denser. There was yellow. There was a beautiful shade of pink, and one that was lighter. There was a white, and it shone brightest. There was a deep purple that was male energy. The orange was female.

Later on, Tracey said that she needed to go on to another color. She said the new color was choosing her:

E: And the orange is choosing you; what is that for?

T: There is a knowledge. It is a strong energy, but in a different way. It's because there are hues of yellow within. Yellow is the knowledge.

E: How do you learn to work with color?

T: I'm just learning to recognize its feeling. You understand. You dissipate your atoms and learn to feel the energy. The energy moves through you.

E: What happens when you work with this orange energy?

T: Creation. Energy is energy. Its application is completely different, but it still creates, and this is something I did not understand at first. It is no less beautiful than blue. I understand its uses and how to apply them. Creativity is quite an exceptional pastime.

E: What do you create?

T: I like to create flowers. The ones I create are orange.

She explained that when she was working with blue energy, she did not create flowers, but worked with healing.

T: Orange is creativity. And I chose to create flowers for and of the earth.

E: Who are you?

T: I am just one of the creators.

E: Where is this learning place? Does it have a name?

T: Everywhere is creation. We go where creation is needed. Now I am with the earth.

E: Did someone give you this task?

T: I chose it. I go where I am needed. You learn through many colors, many schools, through many eons. It's fun! Creating is fun. It is an adventure, putting things together.

E: After creating flowers, what did you create?

T: The trees. There is a strength in the trees that is unknown to many. Specific energies are drawn from the earth itself, but they are different with different trees. They express their individuality very well, better than humans. After the creation of trees, my job is done. I go where I am needed. I don't know where.

Following this interesting conversation, I called forth her higher self and asked what her challenges were:

T: There is still stubbornness in accepting. There is resistance. She thinks things are harder than they are! She achieved. She excelled beyond her expectations, and expectations can often prove to be barriers. She needs to form a door in these barriers. When she sees orange, she will know this is a window of opportunity. She must be willing to walk through it. Orange will be the trigger. She has a preference to learn in these other ways, to feel. This was part of the learning of the energies, learning to feel, but she is happy just learning. It is not necessary to learn through hearing although vibrational tones mean more to her than words.

E: So should she choose the vibrational way of learning?

T: Words are only vibrations. Learning the vibrations of the words will help. If she thinks of them as a sound, she will understand them on a different level.

E: What is her life purpose?

T: It is to continue to create.

E: Create what?

T: To understand the energies, to create different energies—this is inherent in her makeup.

E: How can she remember how to do it?

T: She will start to remember when she walks through the orange door. She needs to remember the creative art time when there was an abundance of energy in everything. And this is the magic in it.

After the session, Tracey reported that she had always been drawn to working with color but did not know how! She said that it was a beautiful feeling when she had learned to know many more colors and was competent in her work. She also said that blue has been her favorite color all her life. Now she knew why.

Chapter 11

Your Intentions Orchestrate Your Life

> *In the movement towards enlightenment, "where you are" is the point of arrival. When you get there, be present for it.*
>
> —Deepak Chopra,
> *Oprah (Winfrey) interviews Deepak Chopra in India*

COMING TO THE PRESENT moment, you get hold of your power and are in a place to focus your attention and intention toward your well-being. Although you can do this anytime, anywhere, the most effective method is a new moon ritual. I developed the habit of writing down all my wishes on the day of the new moon. I always ask that my wishes be granted as long as they are for the highest good of all. I then put this list in a drawer and totally detach from it. Detachment means not thinking about the outcome and releasing all expectations.

I did this exercise with my husband a few years ago, outlining the aspects of our dream house on a piece of paper. Only two months later, our real estate agent called us to say that she had found just the right house for us. Indeed, the house was all we wished for and more. It needed no renovation, since all the required work was taken care of by previous owners!

Affirming our intentions is so powerful that it is important to be cautious, clear, and concise. Two people doing this together create an even bigger spark in consciousness. As long as the wish does not clash with the highest good of the universe, it will be granted in no time. It should not harm another person in any way and should benefit all those affected.

Ultimately, your intentions orchestrate your life. Therefore it is very important to list your desires and turn them into intentions.

There is a subtle working of energies below the surface on the energetic plane. This is beyond the mind's understanding and needs only pointed attention and intention. The rest is an effortless ride requiring only that you to surrender to it. Hermann Hesse puts it beautifully when Siddhartha explains to his lover, "Listen, Kamala, when you throw a stone into the water, it finds its quickest way to the bottom of the water. It is the same when Siddhartha has an aim, a goal. Siddhartha does nothing; he waits, he thinks, he fasts, but he goes through the affairs of the world like the stone through the water, without doing anything, without bestirring himself; he is drawn and he lets himself fall. He is drawn by his goal, for he does not allow anything to enter his mind which opposes his goal." (Hesse, 49)

During my research on the color turquoise, I learned that according to Hindu and Persian mystics, it was very lucky to have a turquoise stone on hand at the time of a new moon. Whoever gazed at the moon on the first day after the new moon and then looked at the stone was destined to enjoy an increase in wealth and protection from evil (Tagore, 2012).

✼✼✼✼✼

Perhaps one of the most interesting sessions on intentions I have had was one with Oya, a lady in her early thirties. Following the initial relaxation, she saw herself as a powerful man, living in a large, beautiful house on a hill overlooking the sea. He was presiding at a business dinner and easily dominated the team of men around the big table. They were all well dressed and hungry for power. Toward the end of the dinner, the man's six-year-old daughter came to say good night.

After dinner, the man felt empty inside and recalled the day he had married his wife. He was tired of being powerful and realized he had been hardened by it. About a year later, he committed suicide, shooting himself in the head. The tragedy was compounded when his daughter entered the room as he pulled the trigger. He felt deep regret and sadness.

When I called forth Oya's higher self and asked why this life and these scenes were shown to her, the answer was that she needed to learn what real strength is. "Real strength is inner strength, not strength on the outside." The man looked strong on the outside, but was weak inside.

Her higher self said, "She is a fighter of light against pure evil. She needs to continue to learn to fight. She is strong; she will do it. She forgets how strong she is, but she will not forget anymore. She ran away from marriage and kids until now, because she wanted to return home to the source quickly. She chose to have a short life and to experience all. She is tired now, and if she chooses, she can live longer and experience her life in a longer period."

My client was overwhelmed by her family, work, and relationship issues and thought it was a punishment to be on earth. I asked how she could have a life of well-being. The answer was, "We will meet to discuss this; she will come as well. She should say she wants this in her earthly life, too! We told her this was too much to experience in such a short time, but she did not listen! We need to hear her consent to stay longer." She was also advised to "hear better." When I asked how she would know she was doing this, my client heard instrumental music. "She will have ringing in the ears when she hears us," was the answer. It is also worth noting that my client came to say goodbye. This was her last time on earth.

The intentions Oya had set before coming to earth were clear and totally orchestrated her life. She chose a short life, but still wanted to experience everything. However, she did not want to get married and have kids because she hoped to return as quickly as possible. Now she wanted to change her life experience.

At the end of the session, her higher self said, "She will have a child!" It was interesting to see the immediate quantum shift when my client changed her intent. On this planet of free will, we create our own reality intention by intention!

Following the session, my client did not remember anything that was said. As we discussed some of the highlights, Oya said she was determined to communicate her consent to stay longer.

I had another deep session regarding intentions with Serap, a lady in her mid thirties. She told me everything was aligned for her to move forward, but she was stuck. She wanted to know what her next steps should be and what was preventing her from moving on. She specifically wanted to know why she had chosen to be here on earth.

When she was relaxed, Serap saw a poor eight-year-old boy, living alone in a cave on a mountain. He went down to the valley and was welcomed and taken home by a wealthy farmer in his thirties, to his happy and crowded farm. The man showed him compassion and fed him, and a fat woman washed him. At dinner, the three were at the head of the table.

When he was eleven years old, five bandits came and killed everyone except for the fat woman, now crippled, and the boy, who hid in an oven. He came out, thinking the bandits were gone. However, one of the bandits saw him and grabbed him. The boy picked up a knife and killed the man in self-defense. Then there was only deep silence and the smell of blood. The boy was traumatized and cried a lot.

In his fifties, he was a top general fighting for his country. However, he was badly wounded, with a spear cutting his gut open. The nurse who took care of him in a tent hospital looked at him with deep compassion. He died, feeling little pain because of the love she showed for him. There was the smell of blood again.

Following his death, a dolphin guide welcomed her. This loving being took her to the bottom of the sea and showed her a giant oyster. The dolphin pointed to the lid with its tail and encouraged her to open the shell. She feared the lid might close on her, so the dolphin stood in between the shells, and she dared to approach. Once the lid was opened, she saw a large, glittering pearl inside that immediately lit up the darkness. "The one who holds this pearl in her hand and looks at it sees the truth," she was told. "You should touch the pearl." She did so. It turned out that the pearl was not solid as she expected, but like compressed gas. "It exists everywhere, but one needs to go deep to find it," she heard. She had dared to go deep within, and following this experience, she was no longer scared of the truth, which she knew existed. Fear was gone! She would show others, too.

When I asked Serap's higher self how all this was connected and what my client should know, the answer was that, "What she lacked in the past life is linked to the pearl. If the man could have felt the light or truth in him, he would not have suffered so much. He could have turned the farm into a loving home again; he would not have given up due to the tragedy. Although he transformed himself into a powerful general, with statues of himself all over the country, love and compassion were missing in his life. His love channels were blocked; he became successful, but unhappy. In her current life, it is the opposite; she will learn to balance. She has no barriers; she should focus on telling the truth she sees. She should ensure others see this as well; she should find the way."

When I asked how Serap could do that, the answer was that she would meet many people around the world. "She should stop doing and just be. She should be comfortable—at peace with herself—like a gypsy. Would a gypsy worry about what others might say?

"She should not be scared. Truth is inside her. That truth spoke out here today. She will go, tell, and make others feel. She should reach out to them! Many people will come into her life.

"Oneness, that pure white energy, is the reality; this should be spread as much as possible. The rest is not important. Tell everyone about the connection, that reality beyond life and death and the life in a human body. When the reality is upside down, there will be no more fear of death. Realities should exchange places. Which reality is really the reality?"

The parting message was, "Love is needed, loving very much."

Following the session, Serap said that all her fears regarding her family and being alone in the water were gone. The next time I spoke to her, she was shining and said she had many ideas about how to share her truth. Her creativity channels were opened wide, and she listened to her intuition more often. Her intention to move ahead and to remove any barriers was immediately heard and honored by the universe.

Chapter 12

From the Angelic Realm

I saw the angel in the marble and carved until I set him free.
—Michelangelo

A FEW OF MY clients channel information that is important to share with you, the awakening beings of the earth. For easy reading, I have compiled the highlights here, clustering them under specific headings. E stands for me and SC for the Superconscious—the angelic realm, as inhabitants call it. You will notice that they have a loving, considerate, but also authoritarian and direct tone. All information given is timeless. They say, "We do not overburden people beyond what they can handle. And we know what to give to whom. We always speak consistently and continue saying these things until people get the message!"

Remembering

E: How can we remember ourselves, our essences? What is most important for humans to know?

SC: Looking within. Journeys are good for everyone. They prepare you for your inner journey.

E: What should we do when we feel low?

SC: Use the water element, going under water or jumping into water. Try the sea or perhaps a pool. Even a bath or shower will do. Water relaxes the vibrations.

E: Will we be able to make it on time?

SC: There is time enough for everything.

E: Why is she so depressed?

SC: She is worrying about her husband too much, but we gave you your lives for yourselves.

On Love

E: How would you define love?

SC: It is like being nothing—nothingness.

E: What should be the priority of a light worker?

SC: Frequency of love. Only this will make your transition easier. Try to get closer to the feeling of nothingness. As you get closer to divine love, everything you see becomes different. Every branch you touch blooms; every word you say echoes, and your tears bloom. You are divine love. Go deeper and deeper until you find this. Humanity will not be saved until this is found.

E: Is this a personal journey?

SC: You cannot reach the whole unless you start at the personal level.

One knows those who walk the path of love. They feel each toe. As you walk, the path is lit up with light. One cannot walk the path to God without burning with love.

As you ascend further, you will hold the hands of those around you and lift them higher. Those who need you will extend their arms to you. Love them very much. As they feel the warmth of love, they will open up like a lotus flower. Continue to gather together, listening to your heart.

Everyone has contracts with each other; make the most of them when your paths cross.

Master souls will always meet somewhere; they will attract and see each other and talk to each other.

Every great soul deserves to listen and to be heard.

E: Why am I sensitive, crying easily?

SC: Because you are on the path of love. Love is warm; it relaxes you. Teardrops cleanse you, like the meeting of water and fire.

Know when to keep your doors locked, since leaving your doors open encourages humans to steal. They may take your belongings or even your energy.

Being a free, independent soul does not mean you should not ask for help.

On the New Age

SC: The coming new age will cleanse you all, enlighten you all, and tie you to each other with love. You will taste hope, happiness, and oneness there.

Good times are coming; however, this won't happen without going deep within to the very bottom. First find the courage to go down deep to the bottom. Then ascension will come. Face your fears. Every fear is forced to disappear when it is touched with the hand.

E: When are the good times coming?

SC: Soon. However, time is not linear, as you know it. You will feel a better time approaching. The enlightened masters will tell you about the approaching time and tell you to prepare. But portals will open within each individual. Individuals will go over to the new age on their own time. Do not be fixated on a certain date or number. The process for opening the heart is different for each created living being. Let go of any worries and relax yourselves. It is not possible to enter the new age by restricting yourselves to templates, numbers, or processes. Just relax. Tell each other what you know, but never forget that all portals will open on their own time, and people will go through those doors on their own and reach enlightenment. When you talk, do not try to make others accept your templates. Share, and hug with love. Act like a lover rather than a teacher.

All people will pass on their own time, with their own steps.

They will complete their journeys. This is why you are here. There is nothing to fear. Satisfy the needs of your body with food, love, and exercise as you feel best. Listen to your inner voice, and you will hear; ways will always be shown.

Exercise helps with the spreading and proper distribution of energy in the body. Then energy works smoothly.

Eat regularly and drink more water. Eat everything, but love what you eat. It is necessary to respect food.

The angelic realm is not as far away as you think. Sometimes it is the person right next to you.

We will all walk together hand in hand in those perfect times when there are endless gardens and light never fades. Water is turquoise, trees are green, and light is with you always. Pick your intentions carefully.

E: What will change in our lives in the coming days; what will we realize?

SC: Enlightenment. The veils of teachings and conditioning over your eyes will be slowly lifted. Guides will teach you how to be brave.

E: How can we help cleanse our loved ones?

SC: We are all responsible for ourselves. Do not be affected by others. Transforming with love is a good method. Surround whatever you want with love and transform it just for you. Everything you see is what you want to see.

You will be the portal yourself. You will leave your bodies, but not as in death. You will be able to go and come back. You will start astral journeys. This will happen more and more.

On Transformation

SC: As you get attached to life on earth, transitions get tougher. Humans should do more meditative work. And we do not ever want fear. We do not know or understand what scares you. If you want to stay on earth, strive to make it a nice place. We are not destructive; we are love. If surrendering and falling in love hurt you, there is nothing to do.

If/as everything is transforming and if/as there are passageways, you will continue to move toward ascension. But why are you fixated on the concept of time? Timing as per what? As you ascend, you will learn to leave behind time and money. If you let this hurt you, it will. Each ending is a beginning, and each beginning an ending. This is how the universe works.

On earth, there is not much to dedicate yourself to. Transferring knowledge may be a good goal. We will not come down flapping our wings and heal the earth; that is a fairy tale. You should find ways to help each other. You are all very precious. Come together and help each other in every way possible.

When you touch a leaf, close your eyes and imagine being that leaf. Imagine it and you become it. You can be the portal. You can pass through the portal and become a light being, a flower, or a car, all within the flow.

When you are quite relaxed, go with the flow of the energies entering your body. Slowly, with each breath, experience the high energy that you absorb. Spread this energy to your whole body, to each cell, erasing the boundaries of your physical self. In this way, you can experience being pure energy. This pure energy can flow into anything, which can then experience that form. With another breath, you can leave that form and return to your old body. As you experience this energy exchange, breath is the most important element, but first comes the intake. Let the life energy enter your body and dissolve the boundaries it sets. Do not worry that you may not return. There is no possibility of that. This is similar to the leaf exercise and different from meditation.

On Uniting

SC: You will continue to grow in number and to come together. The circle will grow bigger, like the ripple created by a pebble thrown in the water. It does not matter where you are in the circle. One vibration will affect the other, this earth, this universe, and others; one pebble is enough to vibrate everything. Those souls who have opened themselves to ascension will continue to come together. We will bring you together; do not worry.

Just seeing, meeting, and knowing each other increase the feeling of unity. It is not necessary that you do something together.

No one is superior to another; hug all humans with love.

A client was experiencing higher and higher realms with each session. I asked, "Each time she goes higher, right?"

SC: She can go to the very bottom, too; this is not a problem. Her ability to go very high does not make her superior to others living on earth.

E: So this is not superiority?

SC: No, because the cosmos is like a sphere. Everything transforms, going up and down. If she cannot be the same with all people she sees and meets on earth, why should we send her there? As long as she is like others, she can be a mirror to them and she can teach them. People live in herds; if they see you as very different from themselves, they will not find you an attractive person to follow.

Love them all; we created all with love. You might judge them, but accept them with love. All souls are divine. Whatever their path on earth is, an assassin, a rapist, or a thief, they all have sacred souls; they can all be trained and are worthy of love. Soften your heart; you may get mad, your mind may be furious, you might snap and shout, but make sure your heart is soft, okay? No living being can stay insensitive to love. The warm, white light emanating from your heart is felt by all living beings. You might be angry at them and slam the door, but as long as your heart continues to love them, you help them, and most of all, you help yourself.

Even the goat, portraying the devil, representing darkness and evil, cannot resist the love in your heart. It might scare you and push you around, but there is nothing to fear. The stronger your love is, the stronger you are. When you live in a vacuum of love, you are struggling, sinking, and drowning.

We would first like you to embrace your parents. You might get mad, be offended, and not approve of their opinions. Still, your heart should bow with love and respect for the energies that carried you to earth. Your behaviors do not necessarily need to show this.

The heart and the mind work together; they balance off. It is all about balance. As your heart gets stronger, your mind gets stronger, and it will think more accurately.

As you get braver, you are filled with love. With more love, frequency increases. When you face problems, go back to the love within you.

The parting message was, "Show more love for everything, without discrimination, without choosing. You might come across anything and everything. As the love in your heart is strengthened, events will be different, your mind will be different, and you will be in contact with different people."

*****

Angels come to help and guide us in as many guises as there are people who need their assistance. Sometimes we see their ethereal, heavenly shadow, bright with light and radiance. Sometimes we only feel their nearness or hear their whisper. And sometimes they look no different from ourselves.

—Eileen Elias Freeman

Chapter 13

Some Unusual Visits

Every time you are tempted to react in the same old way, ask if you want to be a prisoner of the past or a pioneer of the future.

—Deepak Chopra

MY CLIENT WHO CREATED with color (see chapter 10) also said that since her youth, she had felt that she was having animal visitations during her sleep. I asked her higher self if that was right.

SC: Indeed. We are often close by. We come to get her. And we often do this using animals.

E: You get her and take her somewhere?

SC: She comes.

E: To where?

SC: To be creative.

E: She said this happens during the morning hours. Earth time?

SC: It is still dark. She comes, and she creates.

E: What does she create?

SC: Anything that is needed.

E: Just like in that life she saw where she was creating with color?

SC: Yes. This is not forgotten. The memories are never forgotten.

E: Is she doing it now, even in this life?

SC: Yes. When she sleeps, she's creating. She needs to continue that creation into her waking.

In another session, I worked with Taner, a gentleman who was quite intuitive, meditated regularly and loved it. He said in our pretalk that he was interested in discussing anything "nonearthly." He was intrigued by ETs and UFOs and wanted contact.

He was so willing to go under that he was already closing his eyes toward the end of our pretalk. After describing a beautiful place, he reported seeing a whirling dervish.

Once Taner was in a trance state, he saw a big, black spaceship lit up with yellow light. The craft had three or four hexagonal openings that made it look like a honeycomb. "Everything reminds me of bees," he said. "The ship is traveling in space." Then he was inside the ship, greeted by the tall, feminine captain, who said, "You asked to come to us. What do you want?" She took him on a tour of the spaceship and then on a tour of her planet. She had a gentle smile and a human appearance. "The earth on this planet is rusty red, and there are sharp, chimney-type rock formations everywhere, like in Cappadocia." (This is a beautiful area in central Turkey, in the province of Nevsehir.)

E: Why is there so much negative energy on Earth now?
SC: Earth has to go through such a period. He will come here.
E: What is this place called?
SC: Solaris.
E: What is your message to him?
SC: His daughter—to be born—is from Solaris. She is a beautiful girl with smiling eyes, a real angel. She and others are coming to Earth to bring more positivity.
E: What will happen during the shift of Earth?
SC: Earth will be cleansed. The black cloud will be cleaned,

and you will be like us. A long time ago, there was unwanted interference.

E: What should we do during this period?

SC: Turn within. This is nothing physical. Nothing else is important.

E: What is his life purpose?

SC: He is a key, a key for the shift. He is a channel for downloading information, like he is doing now. Be patient.

At this point, they thanked me and I asked Taner to talk to his spirit guide.

E: What is his life purpose?

(Taner saw bright, white light.)

SC: To spread light, to lighten.

E: What is your message to him?

SC: He should not worry about life. No need.

E: How can he remember this in his daily life?

SC: He can feel me.

Obviously, the daughter appeared as his guide! I then called forward his higher self:

E: Why did you show him ETs but no past lives?

SC: He's done with the past; he is ready now. It was time.

E: He is very different from his wife. Why is she in his life?

SC: Because he is from Earth and human.

E: How can he raise his awareness further? Could you please explain with a picture if appropriate?

(He saw a beautiful rainbow, and I asked what this meant.)

SC: Be calm.

E: What changes will he notice in the coming days?

SC: His inner peace will increase.

Neither I nor my client knew anything about Solaris. I did a Google search and asked around about Solaris ("from the sun" in Latin), but came up with little. Then I found "The Councils of Light and the Emergence of the Multi-Dimensional New Earth." It said, "The Solar Council of Solaris: That Being and Body of Light that you call the Sun is now known as Solaris, and it is here that the Solar Council is situated within the Great Solar Council Hall. This is the place where representatives from all the 'planets' and Bodies of Light within the Solaris system gather together to determine their mutual course within the Galactic system."

If people are ready, as in these two cases, they receive such ET information. There are far more cases in which the information is withheld. The main reason is that such knowledge might further distract these people from their purpose in being here. It might be too early for the person to explore that area of his being.

In essence, we are all from the stars, we are all ETs, and we are all from the same source. Information on past lives or lives on other planets is shared only on a need-to-know basis.

On one occasion, my client Emre's higher self said, "We did not show any past lives for his higher good." Later on, it was explained that he did not have any past lives on earth and that he was here to teach. "He knows everything, so he can teach everything." He will eventually be a healer, using his hands. He has a big mission here, but it is not yet time for him to know what it is. He is doing well, though, progressing on his path. This person left corporate life a few years ago and is a wellness instructor. During the trance state, he was traveling in space all the time, experiencing the stars and the planets.

Chapter 14

The Mystery of Dreams

*Spirit is the life, mind is the builder,
and the physical is the result.*

—Edgar Cayce

Right after my first contact with clients, they usually start to have meaningful dreams. This is why I ask them to write down their dreams before coming to a session. During our pretalk, we add these interesting scenes and visions to the question list for their higher selves. In the session, the higher self explains in detail why a client had a particular dream. It is fascinating!

Edgar Cayce called dreams the nightly channel of the higher self. He said we are given dreams from the Superconscious every night. If we have difficulty remembering dreams, a good technique is to take time every morning to record our feelings as soon as we wake up, before getting out of bed. If we don't remember any dreams, we can write whatever comes to mind. Dreams will likely come within a week. Daily meditation is also a proven method for improving dream recall. Most important, we should take action in waking life that reflects or responds to an element in a dream, even in little ways. This brings the dream into the world of the conscious mind.

During sleep, intuition expands while individual consciousness recedes. There is simply being—deep, silent sleep, pure intuition, and pure psychic oneness. At the same time, the Superconscious/

higher self acts as a guardian angel, protecting us in this hyper-receptive state. The soul evaluates life experiences, and this is what we experience as dreaming. Living our soul purposes by aligning ourselves with ideals brings increasingly clear dreams. Furthermore, Cayce encouraged people to seek dreams for guidance, to learn soul purposes, and to safely experience or learn to understand anything we wish.

A simpler way of asking for dream guidance is to write a letter to yourself, asking for advice. Write what you know about a problem and what you intend to do. Ask your dreams to show if there is a better solution, and imagine yourself taking the intended action as you go to sleep with the letter under your pillow. The dreams that follow can be surprisingly helpful (Reed, Chapter 3).

✹✹✹✹✹

Since I find the subject of dreams fascinating, I would like to share some interesting ones recounted by my clients.

Didem was a lady in her forties, and her lesson was to speak her truth at all times to everyone around her. She told me that the night before our session she dreamed that she, her husband, and her two sons were auditioning at a theater. Her husband was given the lead role, and her younger son was chosen as well. However, she and her older son were not selected. When we asked her higher self what this meant, it was explained that she needed to stop acting and start speaking her truth.

Emre had many dreams during the two weeks before our session. In the first series, he always saw himself as a hero, saving many people. His higher self explained that these were shown because he had asked to know his purpose in being here. In another dream, Emre felt corrections in his sacrum area. His higher self explained that Emre's foundation was being strengthened. In another dream, he was about to be hanged, and everyone else was even sadder than he was. He was saved from execution by giving something away. His higher self said that this was symbolic, that he had executed his past and been given a new chance, a new mission. Finally, when Emre asked before going to sleep what work he should do, he dreamed of an old friend who had recently called. His higher self said that Emre might want to work in the area his friend mentioned.

My client Taner told me that he was constantly flying in his dreams. His higher self said that this was related to consciousness ascension.

Here is a dream that had a deep impact on me. As I often do, I asked questions of my higher self before going to sleep. This practice helps me to remember my dreams, the answers, and the signs.

I requested help in finalizing this book. I asked to be shown or sent a writer or someone who would read my work and listen to my words. That night, I dreamed of my father's father, who wrote more than ten published books. He wrote mostly on economic development and died years ago. However, this was moving for me, since I realized I had a strong writer in my blood! That gave me deep confidence at just the time I needed it.

Another interesting nonphysical communication I had around dreams was through Doreen Virtue's Healing with the Angels Oracle cards. I was inspired to draw an angel card, asking, "What is your message to me as I am writing this closing chapter?" To my amazement, out of the forty-four-card deck, I drew the card Dreams!

"Pay attention to your dreams right now. Keep a dream journal," was the message.

Well, since I have been doing that for years, this message is meant for you!

"You are receiving important messages during your dreams. Sometimes you may wake up with the feeling that you have traveled or received instruction during your sleep. You wonder, *why can't I remember my dreams?* The messages and experiences of your dreams are never truly lost or forgotten. They are instead incorporated into your unconscious so that your higher self's wisdom and love govern your actions. You can more easily remember your dreams by writing down whatever you recall immediately upon awakening. Just write any little bit you can remember, and the rest of the dream will unravel your memory. Review your dream journal often, and look for patterns and themes. These recurrent dream issues signify messages that your higher self and the angels are trying to send you." (Virtue, 1999)

Dreams are a wonderful release and communication mechanism between the conscious and subconscious minds, so make use of them. And enjoy the magical worlds, the parallel realities, and your limitless being in action!

Afterword

Spirituality is living your life with an open heart through love.

—Oprah Winfrey

WE ARE ALL SPIRITUAL beings, whether we realize it or not. And experiencing the uniqueness of the spirit is totally dependent on us. Do we allow it to emerge, or do we stick to our routine?

By sharing my journey, I am inviting you to open your mind further so you can flow with life easily and effortlessly.

As new ideas are allowed to enter our awareness, the conditioning of the mind is transcended. This creates the miraculous door for subtle messages from the universe to reach us. Through this door, the energetic orchestration behind the scenes shows its face to us, and we can only admire its perfection. The more flexible we are, the easier it is to transform. The less we plan, the higher the chance that miracles knock on our door.

Practicing and teaching meditation, followed by years of hypnotherapy sessions with my clients, have allowed me to recognize many ways to well-being. I have done my best to share them with you in this book.

Above all, though, I believe each of us is made unique by hearing our inner voice and acting on it bravely.

Therefore I say give your subconscious a chance, allow yourself to speak your truth, and most important, love without discrimination, without choosing!

Reading List

Ambrose, Kala. *9 Life Altering Lessons: Secrets of the Mystery Schools Unveiled.* Foresthill, CA: Reality Press, 2007.

Ambrose, Kala. http://www.exploreyourspirit.com

Calleman, Carl Johan. *The Mayan Calendar and the Transformation of Consciousness.* Rochester, VT: Bear & Company, 2004.

Cannon, Dolores. *Between Death and Life: Conversations with a Spirit.* Huntsville, AR: Ozark Mountain Publishers, 1993.

Cannon, Dolores. *The Keepers of the Garden.* Huntsville, AR: Ozark Mountain Publishers, 1993.

Cannon, Dolores. *The Three Waves of Volunteers and the New Earth.* Huntsville, AR: Ozark Mountain Publishers, 2011.

Chopra, Deepak. *Life after Death: The Burden of Proof.* New York, NY: Three Rivers Press, 2006.

Chopra, Deepak. *The Book of Secrets.* New York, NY: Three Rivers Press, 2004.

Chopra, Deepak. *The Spontaneous Fulfillment of Desire: Harnessing the Infinite Power of Coincidence.* New York, NY: Three Rivers Press, 2003.

Chopra, Deepak and Simon, David. *The Seven Spiritual Laws of Yoga: A Practical Guide to Healing Body, Mind, and Spirit.* Hoboken, NJ: John Wiley & Sons Inc., 2004.

Cooper, Diana Cooper and Hutton, Shaaron. *Discover Atlantis.* London, Great Britain: Hodder & Stoughton, 2005.

Emoto, Masaru. *The Hidden Messages in Water.* Hillsboro, OR: Beyond Words Publishing, 2004. http://www.masaru-emoto.net/english/index.html

Hand Clow, Barbara. *The Mayan Code.* Rochester, VT: Bear & Company, 2007.

Hay, Louise, *You Can Heal Your Life.* Hay House Inc, 1984.

Millman, Dan. *The Life You Were Born to Live. Tiburon, CA:* H. J. Kramer Inc, 1993.

Murphy, Joseph. *The Power of Your Subconscious Mind.* Mansfield Centre, CT: Martino Publishing, 2009.

Newton, Michael. *The Journey of Souls: Case Studies of Life Between Lives.* St. Paul, MN: Llewellyn Publications, 2003.

Norbekov, Mirzakarim. *The Experience of a Fool Who Had an Epiphany about How to Get Rid of His Glasses: Eyesight Restoration is a Simple & Easy Task.* Sofia, Bulgaria: Zhanua '98, 2000.

Osho. *Autobiography of a Spiritually Incorrect Mystic.* New York, NY: St. Martin's Press, 2000.

Peck, Scott. *The Road Less Traveled: A New Psychology of Love, Traditional Values and Spiritual Growth.* Touchstone, 1988.

Spiller Jan. *Astrology for the Soul.* New York, NY: Bantam Books, 1997.

Swami Prabhavananda and Isherwood, Christopher. *Shankara's Crest-Jewel of Discrimination (Viveka-Chudamani).* Hollywood, CA: Vedanta Press, 1975.

Tolle, Eckhart. *A New Earth: Awakening to Your Life's Purpose.* New York, NY: Penguin Group, 2005.

Weiss, Brian. *Many Lives, Many Masters: The True Story of a Prominent Psychiatrist, His Young Patient, and the Past-Life Therapy That Changed Both Their Lives.* New York, NY: Simon & Schuster Inc., 1988.

Works Cited

Andrews, Ted. *Animal-Speak: The Spiritual & Magical Powers of Creatures Great and Small.* St. Paul, MN: Llewellyn Publications, 1997.

Barks, Coleman & Moyne, John. *The Drowned Book: Ecstatic and Earthly Reflections of Bahauddin, The Father of Rumi.* New York, NY: HarperCollins Publishers Inc., 2004.

Beliefnet. *21 Uplifting Angel Quotes.* Accessed September 28, 2012.
http://www.beliefnet.com/Inspiration/Angels/2010/05/21-Uplifting-Angel-Quotes.aspx?p=14

Cayce, Edgar. *Edgar Cayce's A.R.E. Associaton for Research and Enlightenment.*
http://www.edgarcayce.org/are/spiritualGrowth.aspx

http://www.crystalvaults.com/pages/crystal_encyclopedia/turquoise.php

Mowen, John. *Coleman Barks, Rumi Poetry Translation.* Accessed August 22, 2012.
http://www.mowensculpture.com/poetry.html

Chopra, Deepak. *The Seven Spiritual Laws of Success: A Practical Guide to the Fulfillment of Your Dreams.* San Rafael, CA: Amber-Allen Publishing and Novato, CA: New World Library, 1993.

Chopra, Deepak. *Deepa Chopra Quotes.* Accessed October 15, 2012.
http://www.goodreads.com/author/quotes/138207.Deepak_Chopra
http://www.goodreads.com/quotes/633922-when-the-pain-of-being-the-same-becomes-greater-than

Geller, Uri. *The 11:11 Phenomenon.* Accessed August 26, 2012.
http://www.uri-geller.com/articles/11.htm

Gems and Jewels. *Jewel information for you, a Gemstones and Jewelry consumer information encyclopedia.* Accessed in December 2012.
http://www.jewelinfo4u.com/Turquoise_Jewellery.aspx

Hesse, Hermann. *Siddhartha.* London, England: Penguin Books Ltd, 2008.

Life Positive. *Your Complete Guide To Personal Growth. Deepak Chopra - New Age Hero.* Ahhuja, Ajay. Accessed Sept 3, 2012.
http://www.lifepositive.com/Spirit/new-age-catalysts/deepak-chopra/chopra.asp

Lipton, Bruce. *The Biology of Belief.* Santa Rosa, CA: Mountain of Love/Elite Books, 2005.
www.brucelipton.com

Reed, Henry. *Edgar Cayce on Channeling Your Higher Self (Studies in Surface Science and Calaysis).* New York, NY: Warner Books Inc., 1989.

Scott-Kemmis, Judy. *Color Psychology to Empower and Inspire You.* Accessed July 18, 2012.
http://www.empower-yourself-with-color-psychology.com

Tagore, Sourindro Mohun. *Mani-Mala*. Nabu Press, 2012.

The Quotations Page and Michael Moncur. Accessed September 5, 2012.
http://www.quotationspage.com

Thinkexist Quotations. Accessed August 17, 2012.
http://thinkexist.com/quotation/
http://thinkexist.com/quotes/with/keyword/aging/2.html
http://thinkexist.com/quotes/deepak_chopra/2.html

Tooley, Anne Christine. www.energyandvibration.com. Accessed December 25, 2012.
http://www.energyandvibration.com/color.htm

Virtue, Doreen. Healing with the Angels Oracle Cards: *Book and 44-Card Deck by Doreen Virtue* (1999, Cards, Flash Cards)

Yummy Quotes. Life is Supposed to be Delicious. Accessed October 5, 2012.
http://www.yummy-quotes.com/deepak-chopra-quotes.html

Made in the USA
San Bernardino, CA
18 September 2013